Mediators

Mediators

Aesthetics, Politics, and the City

Reinhold Martin

University of Minnesota Press

Minneapolis

An earlier version of chapter 2 was previously published as "Financial Imaginaries: Toward a Philosophy of the City," *Grey Room* 41 (Winter 2010). An earlier version of chapter 3 was previously published as "The Thing about Cities," in *. . . and Materials and Money and Crisis*, ed. Richard Birkett and Sam Lewitt (Vienna: Museum moderner Kunst Stiftung Ludwig Wien, 2013). An earlier version of chapter 4 was previously published as "Public and Common(s)," *Places*, January 2013, http://places.designobserver.com/feature/public-and-commons/37647/.

Published by the University of Minnesota Press
111 Third Avenue South, Suite 290
Minneapolis, MN 55401-2520
http://www.upress.umn.edu

The University of Minnesota is an equal-opportunity educator and employer.

Contents

Forerunners: Ideas First from the University of Minnesota Press

Original e-works to spark new scholarship

Forerunners is a thought-in-process series of breakthrough digital works. Written between fresh ideas and finished books, Forerunners draws on scholarly work initiated in notable blogs, social media, conference plenaries, journal articles, and the synergy of academic exchange. This is gray literature publishing: where intense thinking, change, and speculation take place in scholarship.

Reinhold Martin, *Mediators: Aesthetics, Politics, and the City*

Jussi Parikka, *The Anthrobscene*

John Hartigan Jr., *Aesop's Anthropology: A Multispecies Approach*

Preface

If, as is frequently said, we live in an urbanized age, this is not straight-forwardly so. Events surely crowd the urban stage, even as boundaries melt, edges soften, and centers disperse. But history has pulled the rug out from under the modern metropolis and its myths, in place of which creeps an aestheticized confusion as to what happens, exactly, when we use "city" to denote a zone of human habitation that is indeterminate by its very nature. I mean "aestheticized" in Nietzsche's sense, as a physio-logical effect of and on the body politic, a body that constitutes and is constituted by that zone. And I mean "indeterminate" in that, as numbers pile up into facts, it becomes that much more difficult to distinguish the city as a realm of freedom from the winter palace of a bloated, shape-less new sovereign. An overwhelming sense awe at the inhuman scale and pace of it all casts a long shadow across the pathway by which the polis leads to the political. That pathway ramifies in many directions, all of which compel thought.

The five public and pedagogical essays collected here take note of some problems that arise when the city—any city, but also, any *particular* city—becomes a thing with which to think. By this I mean a component in our cognitive infrastructure, a piece of a material complex that is both a way of knowing the world and a thing to be known in its own right. I describe these essays as "public and pedagogical" because they all orig-inated in attempts to think with others about cities, in lecture halls and classrooms, out loud. As a subset of a series, they compile notes toward a theory of the contemporary, globalized city at the crossroads of aesthetics and political economy. Each essay touches on specific mediators, or infrastructural, technical, and social systems that condition experience, delimit the field of action, and partition knowledge. These mediators can be statistical reports, urban–rural transactions, slum relocation schemes, iconic buildings, iron cages and steel shells, social housing, ruined libraries, satellites, or the rough, reddish landscape of Mars. They differ from the "media" of classical media theory in that they are not exactly or not only technological instruments or systems, but they are not so much more as to include everything under the sun. And they differ from the "mediations" accomplished by culture, money, language, and other intervening layers in certain Marxisms, in that their logic is not always reducible to that of capital, even in the last instance. In fact, at times capital's logic reduces down to theirs.

The essays partially record over a decade of teaching and speaking on the subject and its histories, during which time the conversation has unfailingly returned to the question "What is a city, today?" The voluminous literature on contemporary cities has answered that question in rich, empirical detail. Some has given lasting shape to such figures as the "global city," "splintering urbanism," and other durable categories that both describe and interpret widespread phenomena.[1] Some has reversed the arrow and probingly explored the "urban imaginaries" that condition historical and present-day understandings of political, economic, and social life.[2] Relatively little, however, has put the two together, and treated the aesthetic and imaginary life of cities as a determining factor in their political economy, as input for their networked infrastructures (as well as their output), or, for that matter, as a key to rethinking the polis itself. These essays develop that proposition in the mixed, incomplete, and sometimes incommensurable language of media theory, political theory, and aesthetics, with the occasional help of telltale architectural or urban fragments.

Today's cities are built on massive cracks. A widening gulf between wealth and poverty divides populations worldwide, both on the ground and in the social and cultural imagination. Differentials of race, class, and gender crisscross this divide, cutting new crevices, and occasionally building bridges. These differentials, and the fissures and bridges they entail, are without exception enacted by mediators: material bodies, infrastructures, things.

In general, the mediators and their political–economic entanglements observe the laws of the double bind.[3] That is, they enable one set of possibilities while disabling another, equally plausible one, by delineating the horizons within which thought and action take place. In doing so, they reproduce the no-win scenarios of the double bind by appearing to reconcile mutually exclusive possibilities in a manner that is far more intractable than any ordinary contradiction. For in the end, the latter takes up primary residence on the logical (or ideological) plane, rather than on the practical or performative plane occupied by the double bind. But knots can be cut and binds can be unwound, albeit with difficulty. Each of the essays tries its hand at this, by reminding the reader that the rules of the world game are usually not on the table. In examining objects, systems, processes, and imaginaries that weave the double binds of the city, each essay annotates a fragment of the recursive globe on which the particulars of any city revolve. Together, I hope that these annotations amount to something like an excerpt from an unfinished recording, rehearsed but not, for that very reason, definitive. To be repeated, like exercise—or teaching.

Notes

1. Saskia Sassen, *The Global City: New York, London, Tokyo* (Princeton: Princeton University Press, 1991); Stephen Graham and Simon Marvin, *Splintering Urbanism: Networked Infrastructures, Technological Mobilities and the Urban Condition* (New York: Routledge, 2001); as well as the work of David Harvey.

2. Andreas Huyssen, ed., *Other Cities, Other Worlds: Urban Imaginaries in a Globalizing Age* (Durham: Duke University Press); Arjun Appadurai, *Modernity at Large: Cultural Dimensions of Globalization* (Minneapolis: University of Minnesota Press, 1996); Gyan Prakash, *Mumbai Fables* (Princeton: Princeton University Press, 2010).

3. On the double bind: Gregory Bateson, *Steps to an Ecology of Mind* (New York: Ballantine, 1972). More recently: Gayatri Chakravorty Spivak, An Aesthetic Education in the Era of Globalization (Cambridge: Harvard University Press, 2012).

City, Country, World

In some domains, like economics or urban sociology, the preeminence of number and the reign of a numerical imaginary occasionally underwrites a comfortable self-evidence, the decoding of which has largely become the province of the humanities. Add to this the question of sovereignty, of individual subjects, nations, classes, and other units or groupings, and the stakes rise. The city, as territory, as infrastructure, or as image, is no less determined by the foundational indeterminacies of counting than it is reliably fixed in space and in time as a knowable entity.

The problem of scale, which is only potentially numerical, allows us to grasp this. Thinking about cities, about their physical fabric, their histories, their monuments, the forms of life they do and do not support, and the meanings they do and do not convey is native, so to speak, to architectural studies, which is where I will begin but not where I will end. As an architectural matter, putting cities and numbers together helps get at the elusiveness of scale, as well as at the bearing that scale and scalability have on the political and economic imagination. I say scale and not size, since, where size is easily made to seem absolute, and independent of historical experience, scale is an inherently relative concept that bears all the burdens of time, place, and epistemological specificity.

Think, for example, of the dictum commonly associated with the fifteenth-century Florentine humanist Leon Battista Alberti: "the city is like some large house, and the house is in turn like some small city."[1] Returned to its context in the first book of Alberti's *De Re Aedificatoria* (*On the Art of Building in Ten Books*, 1452), in which the author describes the lineaments, or the design elements, of a well-conceived house, this statement is less tautological than it initially sounds. Attributing the insight to unnamed philosophers, Alberti compares the rooms of a house to "miniature buildings" comprising an idealized city, or what he elsewhere calls a "single, integral, and well-composed body."[2] We commonly recognize this as the geometrical body of Renaissance humanism, abstracted and proportionately scaled up as an instrument of quasi-secular authority. From Alberti to Le Corbusier, the well-delineated house reflects that body's scalar range. But what secures the house's integrity in this famous passage is its comparability to a city, while what secures the city's integrity is its comparability to a house.

In Alberti's day, as for centuries before, the European city's actual security and hence its integrity was typically guaranteed by the walls and other barriers, like moats, that surrounded it. His "city" was still a city-state, like the Florence of the Medicis or the Rome of Nicholas V, to whom Alberti presented his treatise. In this respect, enclosure, rather than measure, proportion, or scalar coordination, is the first prerequisite for the political, economic, and psychic security promised by the city–house analogy. Rather than necessarily reproducing some anthropocentric ideal, however, the analogy merely recognizes the prerequisite of tangible spatial boundaries as a condition for sovereignty.

But you would already have suspected the simplest of pseudohistorical narrative traps, in which standard-issue humanist types sally forth onto modernity's stage as straw figures of the sovereign subject and its institutions, only to be undercut by their own discursivity, if not replaced entirely by new and more robust figures, like the capitalist body-without-organs. In fact, my purpose in summoning the Albertian city-as-house is the contrary: to invoke, in a kind of historical shorthand, the durability of a type of sovereignty associated with enclosure, that is conserved rather than dismantled with what the political theorist Wendy Brown, echoing many others, has called the "waning" of the nation-state.[3]

For Brown, walls that enclose or divide nations, such as the six-hundred-mile-long fence erected at the U.S.–Mexico border, or the wall that divides Israel from Palestine, are paradoxical emblems of what she calls "sovereign failure." Rather than confirm or consolidate the national space, they enact or perform an exaggerated sovereignty even as the integrity of the nation-state is undermined by economic globalization and neoimperialism, as well as by networks of non-state actors of all kinds. From this follows a tense dialectic of economy and security, or destabilizing flows and overcompensating enclosures: deterritorialization and reterritorialization without end. I think Brown is right about this; but I also think that her central paradox is overly dependent on the centuries-old association of sovereignty with enclosure with which I began.

Scaled up from house to city to nation, and back down again, this concatenation of spaces provides the infrastructure for jarring encounters between the phantasms of "homeland security" and "free trade" familiar to every airline passenger whose less-than-ideal body, positioned with legs spread and arms outstretched like Da Vinci's Vitruvian man, has been penetrated by the electromagnetic radiation of a millimeter wave scanner; or, much more urgently, to those migrant workers, subjects of the North American Free Trade Agreement, who are regularly hunted down by vigilantes in the desert borderlands of the American southwest. Even so, rather than merely residing comfortably in a single skin, each of these individuals, grouped and divided along multiple axes, is an unstable number, a unit in a pulsating calculus for which enclosed spaces are the equivalent of numerical sets, and identities are variables in a parametric equation.

The same goes for cities. Any city can be described numerically, but the world picture that emerges is quite different from the relational, visibly bounded Albertian city-as-house. A seemingly absolute numerical scale, rather than nested, relational scales of enclosure, guides the terminology we typically use to name different types of conurbation: town, city, megacity, and so on. Consequently, problems arise when the city begins to appear boundless, and it becomes more difficult to attribute to it a reliable scale relative to the individual human body, the primary unit by which cities have heretofore been measured. When that unit is multiplied and split into variables and codes, there arises a fierce conflict between the absolute and the relative, or the universal and the particular, which is the proper domain of urban studies.

This conflict affects even the nonchalant listing of quantitative information in technical manuals. It shows up, for example, in such unlikely places as the influential United Nations–HABITAT *State of the World's Cities* reports, begun in 2001 and issued every two years since. These reports document the rise of the world's megacities and associated conurbations, with an emphasis on the vulnerability of impoverished urbanites and strategies for addressing that vulnerability. The reports are therefore both descriptive and normative in character. They are also the source for the oft-repeated claim that "half of humanity [or half the world's population] now lives in cities."

This claim was first made in the introduction to the fourth, 2008–2009 UN report by Anna K. Tibaijuka, the UN under-secretary-general and executive director of UN–HABITAT. In his foreword to the same document, UN Secretary-General Ban Ki-moon echoed Tibaijuka's assertion, thereby lending to it the full authority of a world body entrusted with imparting meaning to such statements. The previous report in the UN series, from 2006–2007, set the stage, by pointing out rather melodramatically that "sometimes it takes just one human being to tip the scales and change history. At some point in the year 2007, that human being would either move to a city or be born in one," marking the moment when, for the first time, a majority of humans live in cities.[4]

The same report (from 2006–2007) rather more quietly pointed out that what is meant here by "city" is highly counterintuitive. With a strong whiff of redundancy, that report's opening paragraph observes that "cities, whether small municipalities of 2,000 inhabitants or massive agglomerations of 10 million people or more, are becoming a widespread phenomenon," thereby collapsing vastly different spaces and forms of life into a single, ambiguous category—"city"—with indeterminate boundaries.[5] Matters become even more muddled when a methodological note acknowledges that, although the UN has its own criteria for defining an "urban agglomeration," a "metropolitan area," or a "city proper," global demographic generalizations are ultimately dependent on classifications that vary nationally. In other words, the technical definition of a "city," according to the United Nations, is a governmental function that varies significantly from state to state. For example, as of 2003 one hundred and five countries based their definition on what are called "administrative criteria," such as spatial boundaries; one hundred countries "define[d] cities by population size or population density," with some minimums as low as two hundred inhabitants; twenty-five countries emphasized "economic characteristics" in their definitions (such as, for example, "the proportion of the labour force employed in non-agricultural activities"); eighteen countries used criteria that include the "availability of urban infrastructure"; twenty-five countries "offer[ed] no definition at all"; and six countries "count[ed] their entire population as urban."[6]

I am not concerned with the accuracy or inaccuracy of the resulting statistics; I am concerned with the world picture thus conjured. To be precise, it is possible that in 2007 someone moved to or was born in a small town—or even a village—somewhere in the world, thus tipping the scales of the dominant historical narrative in the direction of an underspecified and overdetermined "urbanization," wherein half the world's population was now deemed by a variety of inconsistent, national criteria to be living in "cities." There are of course many practical reasons for the demographic artifice—not the least of which is the assessment, again clearly stated, that due to their density and connectivity, classically urban areas offer the best opportunities for meeting some of the UN's Millennium Development Goals. Exaggerating the shape of urbanization potentially increases the chances of success by attracting attention and resources to a worldwide crisis. As Tibaijuka says in the 2007 report, the improvements in water and sanitation accessible to megacity slum dwellers, for example, can have a "knock-on" efficiency in terms of health, nutrition, and environment that is less easily attainable in more sparsely populated areas.[7] So in part, the UN reports dramatize the pseudohistorical event of a majority urban population partly to highlight long-standing trends that have become desperately exacerbated, and partly to indicate that cities, as ever, offer more bang for the buck.

Buried in all the equivocation, however, is what Raymond Williams called a "structure of feeling" in which, as Williams cogently predicted, the long-standing urban–rural antagonism and interdependency has entered a new phase. Although he later elaborated the expression more fully, in *The Country and the City* (1973) Williams uses "structure of feeling" to describe, among other things, the imaginary association of the rural idyll and other "illusory ideas of the rural past" with childhood.[8] Within such a frame, urbanization is equivalent to a coming of age; it is therefore not difficult to read in the technocratic language of the United Nations reports an infantalization of the dispossessed that Williams associated with capitalist expansion, including imperialism.

These two UN reports, like the two that preceded them and the two that followed, exhibit an undeniable formalism in their arguments that reinforces such a structure. This formalism is characterized by symmetries of various sorts, beginning with the urban–rural polarity itself. In the predominantly numerical language of the reports, it is as if a primordial asymmetry has been overcome. Having reached the statistical halfway point, by whatever dubious means, the "city" now equals if not surpasses the "country" as the natural ground for human life.

This is not to say that naturalized metropolitan narratives necessarily take the place of the rural idyll—or what Western architectural theory has long called the "primitive hut"—in hegemonic discourse. On the contrary, these UN reports and many other documents like them emphasize the precariousness of life in urban slums. In doing so, however, they transpose the older, aestheticized pathos of rural European poverty onto this new figure of "the city," which is to be carefully distinguished from its early twentieth-century predecessors, such as the Großstadt or metropolis. For though the "structure of feeling" associated with these earlier figures entailed a certain precariousness of its own, this precariousness was consistently moored to bourgeois futurity. In the modern metropolis, the removal of certainties, along with psychic and economic insecurity, was oriented toward an open future in which contradictions would progressively resolve, material conditions would rebalance, and the deracinated subject would find a home in the world. As the history of twentieth-century architecture and urbanism in Europe, North America, East Asia, and the colonial and postcolonial South abundantly demonstrates, classical modernist topoi such as abstraction, estrangement, and the uncanny (*unheimlichkeit,* or unhomeliness) were never ends in themselves, but stopping points, or "waystations" (as the Soviet artist–architect El Lissitzky used to say) en route to a new organic synthesis. Hence the confidence with which even a thinker as alert as Friedrich Engels could associate rural-to-urban migration with revolutionary transformation in his treatment of the European housing question.

No longer captivated by the master narrative of techno–social integration, the formalism embedded in the statement "half of humanity now lives in cities" tends to neutralize such futurity while reproducing internally its teleological premises. We are meant to gasp in sublime horror at the assertion, without pausing to ask about the other half, or to wonder at the arbitrary significance of the supposed tipping point. Given the ambiguities involved in actually defining a city, and given the imagined association of the rural with infantalized, precapitalist life, the statement could also be read as indicating, with due alarm, that even today, *only* half of humanity fully participates in capitalist *Bildung,* or personal growth, a process that culminates in urbanization.

The contrary, of course, is one of Williams's main points throughout his remarkable book. The rural, including the imagined rural idyll as the childhood home of humanity, was an integral part of industrial capitalism from the start. In each of its phases, Williams argues, European (in his case, principally British) capitalism reorganized, expropriated, and idealized the agrarian countryside and later, the colonial and postcolonial "hinterlands," as a site of resource extraction, a source of labor, and an object of aesthetic contemplation. As I have said, many of the reports in the UN series, which began with a study of the urban consequences of accelerated globalization, emphasize the outpacing of rural poverty by its urban equivalent, which is most visible in slums and other types of squatter settlements. In these settlements, it is as if the destitution of a rural landscape, deprived by industrial expansion of its historical means of subsistence, has been reproduced in ramshackle shantytowns that sit check-by-jowl with luxury residential high-rises, corporate offices, and public spaces otherwise populated by the working and middle classes.

Without saying so, the UN reports thus tend to describe the ensuing crisis in terms that reproduce the earlier urban–rural partition. Global, regional, national, and municipal data are gathered and displayed in such a way as to blend the village, farm, or small town and their landscapes into an archaic background against which the historical drama of urbanization plays out. Urban destitution shows up as a sort of remainder, a burden of the hinterlands now moved into the city. And yet we know perfectly well, and Williams persistently points out, that during the modern period restructurings of the relations of production are always both agrarian and mercantile/industrial in character.

Such restructurings are also the matrix from which an aesthetics of "modern life" developed in European and North American cities during the late nineteenth century. Despite their frequent revolutionary tone, the aesthetic programs of the modernist avant-gardes tended to reproduce the categorical separation of the rural and the urban and its accompanying hierarchies. Exemplary here are the vivid portraits of nineteenth-century Paris that the urban economist David Harvey elicits from the novels of Balzac, and that the art historian T. J. Clark elicits from the paintings of Manet. Both mention the city's outskirts, or what Clark calls its "environs," but neither does much to analyze the coproduction of an aesthetics of fleeting instabilities with that of rural stasis, a coproduction revealed by the countryside around London mapped by Williams through the literature and poetry of the same period. For both Harvey and Clark, city is to country as figure is to ground, active is to passive, and future is to past; for Williams, the two are locked in a struggle of mutual construction, in which the hegemony exercised by modern metropolitan life and industrial capitalism is fundamentally dependent on the active reorganization of the rural, both in the imagination and on the ground.

In these kinds of situations, as in the UN reports, aesthetics has a way of imperceptibly trading places with political economy. The numbers in which the reports are grounded, including their visualization in graphs, charts, and tables, speak with awe and terror of dynamic, uncontrolled urban growth around which boundaries can no longer be drawn. Brought to life by these sober statistics, the city roils and pulsates like a churning vortex that draws everything irresistibly toward itself. Inside the vortex, the ruins of the Parisian barricades seem to reappear, as the dispossessed struggle for what several of the reports call, with shades of Harvey and of Henri Lefebvre, their "right to the city." But in the language of the United Nations, this "right" stops short of social and economic equity, or even full access to the resources generated and consumed by the great urban engine. Instead, it merely requests recognition and treatment as proper representatives of the urban "poor" who now occupy the place in the metropolitan imagination formerly held by impoverished farmers. This is a right, for example, to move about—but not to live in—the same streets, parks, and "public" amenities as the wealthy, but not necessarily to sit in the same classrooms, be cared for in the same hospitals, or sleep in the same buildings.

The accompanying reduction of the "city"—however that category is defined by governmental discourse—to a shared amenity, or to a sort of generalized streetscape shared by day but not by night, resurfaces in another, surprising form in the 2012–2013 UN report. That report, which seeks to measure the impact of the Arab uprisings, the Occupy movement, and other revolts against the dominant order, reintroduces the figure of the urban "commons." Not exactly the commons as reimagined by Michael Hardt and Antonio Negri, the commons invoked by the 2012–2013 report is roughly equivalent to the natural, social, and informational "environment," the air flowing through city streets, the water in its pipes, the grass in its parks, and the bits in its networks.

Buried more deeply in such references are historical objects and events, principally in this case the common manorial lands cultivated by English farmers according to a complex system of shared husbandry, right up to the early nineteenth century. In a parliamentary process that began in the late sixteenth century, these lands were gradually subject to "enclosure," or expropriation by landowning elites. It is possible, then, that the unenclosed agrarian commons offers an exemplary, potentially repeatable instance of mutuality, communal production, and self-management—a type of open, rural alternative to the walled city-state. However, while acknowledging its many virtues, Williams, in another anticipatory gesture, observes the retrospective tendency to isolate the unenclosed lands from the class structures and other socioeconomic relations in which they were historically embedded. Referring to the example of open-field villages, Williams avers that "we must be careful not to confuse the techniques of production—the open-field strips—with what can easily be projected from it, an 'open' and relatively equal society."[9] Citing a detailed historical account of one such village, he concludes that its social structure was, in miniature, "not, at first sight, so dissimilar from the social structure of mature rural capitalism as to suggest a radically different social order," composed as it was of a local gentry, small entrepreneurs, and the propertyless poor. The rights to common resources of the laborers and tradespeople making up such a population were various and sometimes marginal. Yet they did guarantee a degree of independence and, as Williams puts it, "an important protection against the exposure of total hire."[10] Mutuality was therefore both conditional and genuine, but it was not enclosure alone that sealed its fate. Rather, a whole sovereign system of production and ownership, accompanied by the new symbolic order of the country houses and estates, was in formation. The parliamentary enclosure of common lands was, as Williams says, a contributing factor, but it was not the whole story of the conversion of rural life-in-common into what he calls a "community of the oppressed," and the invention, in effect, of a correspondingly new and separate class: "the poor."[11]

Through the course of the twentieth century, this historically determined figure, the rural "poor," has reappeared in different guises as a harbinger of crisis in the heart of the great European and North American metropolises and, more recently, in postcolonial megacities. In each case, the crisis has been real. As is well documented in the UN reports, widespread, desperate poverty, starkly contrasting with ostentatious, predatory wealth, has been a predominant feature of many contemporary cities. But numbers are also bearers of affect and organizers of the perceptual and cognitive field, by means of reproducible "structures of feeling" such as that which positions the material indices of urban poverty in relation to the repressed history of the rural.

How does this work? Although their units of enumeration are ultimately individual human bodies, rounded off to the nearest million or half million, the epistemic unit of the UN reports is actually the nation-state. When the time comes to issue recommendations in response to the thoroughly documented crises, each of the reports seeks to balance the leverage available to national governments with the contextual nuance available to local or municipal authorities. Likewise with the data themselves. It is, after all, the disparate demographic policies and practices of individual national bureaucracies that paint the ambiguous picture of half of humanity living in cities in the first place.

This default to national sovereignty runs counter to recent trends in which transnational networks of major and minor cities tend to form their own coherent, semi-sovereign "spaces" of economic and cultural exchange. Like the high-speed rail lines that often subtend them, these networks stretch across the intervening countryside without really entering it.[12] Even when limited to a single nation, linked cities do not necessarily inhabit the same governmental space as their surroundings, saturated as they are by development and tax incentives, as well as by infrastructure and services. Although they largely ignore these external linkages, the UN reports do follow many urban scholars in describing cities "divided" or fragmented internally along economic as well as ethnic lines. While these divisions sometimes coincide with actual and virtual walls breaking up an otherwise continuous urban field into segregated zones or pockets, in reality they are divisions among different, competing sovereignties that may or may not occupy the same space—an example of which are the "poor" themselves, subjects of urban crisis dispossessed not necessarily of a idyllic, rural world they might otherwise have held in common, but of their status as historical actors. Described in the language of statistics, these latter-day "wretched of the earth" are no longer subjects of a city divided along classically colonial lines (as they were for Frantz Fanon) to whom national emancipation remained an available option. Instead, they are simply the universal "poor," persons-without-qualities whose enforced—although certainly not actual—silence and anonymity are offset, pragmatically, by the tireless efforts of bureaucrats and academics alike to insist on the situatedness of destitution, by breaking down the numbers nationally and subnationally—often, as in the UN reports, with the help of colorful narrative vignettes highlighting cultural difference.

The one narrative element that is systematically absent from these reports and from the discourse that organizes them is a structural analysis and critique of transnational capitalism itself. In its place are tautological observations regarding the "irony" that a strong central government, whether democratic or authoritarian, offers the best route to what are frequently referred to as "pro-poor" urban reforms. Doubling that irony, in the report published immediately before the Arab uprisings of 2011, the governments of Egypt and Tunisia were among the highest ranked in terms of such initiatives.[13]

As witnessed in the political struggles that followed the revolutions in those two countries, what Brown calls the "waning" (but not disappearance) of post-Westphalian state-based sovereignty also entails, in her account, both the desublimation of religious feeling previously contained in the secular state, and the ontotheological emergence of capital as a new, *global* sovereign."[14] A key feature of this twin process, which reads in Brown's argument as both cause and effect, is the displacement of Hobbesian "awe," which partially underwrote the state's authority, onto walled monuments to weakened borders. Brown characterizes the theatrical quality of these otherwise redundant or futile walls as performatively theological, in the sense that the walls enact, often in an exaggerated manner, the very futility and obsolescence of the enclosure that they also monumentalize.

There is, however, another, related way to think about the decline of the state's constitutive aura. As Brown reminds us, this decline does not lead to secularization, whether at the hands of capital or at the hands of a transnational polity. Rather, it leads in part to what she calls a "theological political sovereignty," authorized by explicit religious belief or by theologies of the market rather than by the awe elicited by a Godlike, secular Leviathan. Political decisions, including those concerning life and death, cannot therefore be thought of as autonomous or prior to economic or religious matters. However, in light of our discussion of enumeration, rather than retain, as Brown does, the Schmittian formulation of the sovereign as "he who decides" in a Godlike manner on the friend–enemy relation, it is possible to rephrase the sovereign as "the one who counts." And I mean this in both senses, of the one doing the counting and the one who is counted.

In the earlier forms of what Michel Foucault called governmentality, which culminated, for example, in Adolphe Quetelet's refinement of statistics as a social science, the arts of governing and the arts of counting occupied one and the same space, which was that of the nation-state. Something similar can be said in microcosm (in other words, at an internally related scale) about the great, wall-less metropolises that emerged in Europe and the United States during the same period. New, statistically oriented disciplines such as urban planning and sociology were closely tied to the territorial integrity of the city as a locus of social reform, and to the state in which that city was located. Whether this reform was initiated by the state or by private actors is less important than the fact that the state or the municipality was the primary medium through which biopolitical data were produced and gathered, as shown, for example, by the technical, social, and political significance of the national census.

As we have seen, when the city overspills its boundaries the state does not cede all its enumerative functions to extranational or transnational entities. On the contrary, these entities, including the United Nations as well as such organizations as the World Bank and the International Monetary Fund, assimilate often incommensurable state-specific data into master narratives, such as that of global urbanization, that *do not* merely represent a proportional scaling up of sovereign, bounded space from house to city to country to world. Instead, such narratives—like the one that reads "over half of humanity now lives in cities"—reproduce a form of *awe* specific to the sovereign, and only the sovereign, who counts. The best approximation of this awe remains what Immanuel Kant called the "mathematical sublime." As Kant puts it, "We call *sublime* what is *absolutely large*"—that is, "something large beyond comparison," or in the terms we have been using, something with size, or magnitude, but no scale.[15] Mathematically, Kant describes this magnitude in crypto–theological terms as "equal only to itself," present not in nature but in ideas (or "the imagination") alone. In short, Kant's mathematical sublime arises only as an unsubstantiated but non-arbitrary judgment for which, as he says, *"that is sublime in comparison with which everything else is small."*[16]

This is the performative aspect of the "over half" in the statement "over half of humanity now lives in cities." The city, unbound from its walls and from its dialectic with the countryside, even as it reproduces these inside and out, is no longer a finite, sensible object, the scale of which is determined by comparison to a house, and vice versa. Having crossed the anthropocentric threshold, it has lost its unit of measure and become an object of what Kant calls the "supersensible," a state of mind grasping toward the absolute. As such, it can be measured but not contained, its inhabitants counted but without certainty. This state of mind, this counting without end, constitutes the new sovereignty. Like the urban, which has not erased or superseded its old antagonism with the rural but rather internalized it in the form of an unaccountable "poor," this new sovereign does not rule over enclosures. It operates in the open, in the indeterminate zone where houses and worlds meet. It secures and protects its subjects first by counting them, not with transcendent fixity but as variables, infinitely divisible units with a potentially endless series of properties. It is not surprising, then, that the United Nations reports, which explicitly aim for social justice, do not contain a structural critique of the mutations in transnational capitalism to which many of the urban crises they list can be traced. This is not merely because capital is the new sovereign. It is because such a critique would be a critique of mathematics itself—not of its truth value, but of its capacity to convey the theological content that all sovereignties require. Such a critique cannot be limited to the sciences or the social sciences. It can only be undertaken within the domain of aesthetics.

Notes

1. Leon Battista Alberti, *On the Art of Building in Ten Books*, trans. Joseph Rykwert, Neil Leach, and Robert Tavernor (Cambridge: MIT Press, 1998), 23.

2. Ibid., 24.

3. Wendy Brown, *Walled States, Waning Sovereignty* (New York: Zone Books, 2010).

4. United Nations Human Settlements Programme (UN–HABITAT), *The State of the World's Cities Report, 2006/2007: 30 Years of Shaping the Habitat Agenda* (London: Earthscan, 2006), "Overview," iv.

5. Ibid., 6.

6. Ibid., "Defining 'Urban,'" 7.

7. Ibid., introduction, iii.

8. Raymond Williams, *The Country and the City* (New York: Oxford University Press, 1973). On "structures of feeling" see also Williams, *Marxism and Literature* (New York: Oxford University Press, 1977), 128–35.

9.   Williams, *The Country and the City*, 102.

10.   Ibid.

11.   Ibid., 104.

12.   See Neil Brenner, *New State Spaces: Urban Governance and the Rescaling of Statehood* (New York: Oxford University Press, 2004).

13.   UN–HABITAT, *The State of the World's Cities Report, 2008/2009: Harmonious Cities* (London: Routledge, 2013), 186.

14.   Brown, *Walled States, Waning Sovereignty*, 64.

15.   Immanuel Kant, *Critique of Judgment*, trans. Werner S. Pluhar (Indianapolis: Hackett, 1987), 103.

16.   Ibid., 105.

[2]

Financial Imaginaries

The aesthetic life of cities entails a volatile mixture. For over a century, the social relations of the metropolis have been linked analytically to financial circulation, a connection that is clearly audible in the term "global city." This applies both in the narrow, deterministic sense that would privilege techno–economic development as causal, as well as in the broader, more inclusive sense that would assign to social, cultural, and aesthetic processes a semi-structural role in shaping the pulsations and interchanges of economic life. In either sense, the city stands as a receptacle, a sort of archaeological site for holding these dynamics in place long enough and firmly enough to study them in all their complexity.

This scenario was inherited in part from the great thinkers of modern, metropolitan experience—from Georg Simmel to Max Weber to Walter Benjamin, with Marx and Engels just over the horizon. Their cities, Berlin and Paris, with London, Moscow, and New York hovering outside the frame, gave the term "metropolis" its phenomenological texture. For his part Benjamin, reading Charles Baudelaire, was able to imagine the Parisian arcades as paradigmatic of the circulation of both commodities and dream images through the interstices of "modern life," primarily through the literary device of allegory. This insight would eventually be inverted and transformed in that same city into the Situationist *dérive*, with the help of which a later cohort of urban thinkers, from Henri Lefebvre to Michel de Certeau, would draw their lines in the sand: *sous les pavés, la plage*.

But this tradition, which extracted general principles from what late twentieth-century urbanists called the "historical center" of European cities (for which the barricades of May 1968 now appear as an ironic emblem), has become a quaint, if not entirely irrelevant, vantage point from which to approach the "world around" dynamics of today, to borrow a term from the idiosyncratic lexicon of R. Buckminster Fuller. Fuller can stand here as a late representative of the counterproposition, incipient in modern architecture and urbanism and thoroughly manifest in midcentury modernization discourse and its policies and practices, that the metropolis was a node in a much larger network that could only be apprehended from above. Just as the inside-out, bottom-up view of the city and of modernity in general, from Benjamin to the Situationists, was enabled by technologies of perception that ranged from the reading glasses of the dandified, pedestrian flâneur, to the plate glass in which the arcades were enclosed, to the vividly painted panoramas that destroyed perspective and enfolded distant horizons, so too did the aerial, eventually planetary view have its technical media. These also had partial roots in the European nineteenth century, in aerial photography (as Benjamin intuited), and in imperial cartography, but they would be fully expressed only in the multiscreen, computerized war rooms of the Cold War, mirrored in the control rooms of the American National Aeronautics and Space Administration (NASA) or the Russian Soyuz program, and eventually miniaturized in geographic information systems and Google Earth.

Historically, our two vantage points, from the street and from the control room, develop simultaneously rather than in sequence. Though we might, therefore, be tempted to assign to each a valence—negative for the dominating, leveling perspective from above; positive for the situated, everyday perspective from below—and hence to oppose them as two terms in a dialectic of modernization, we would do better to recognize the inherent limitations of the analytical frame thereby described.

This requires a theorization of media that exchanges the eschatology of a McLuhan—or, for that matter, the millenarianism of a Baudrillard or a Virilio—for a materialism descended from Foucauldian archaeology, but with an emphasis on infrastructural systems and artifacts in which ways of seeing and ways of knowing are coproduced. Such a perspective supersedes the endgame that opposes the street to the control room. Far from harboring a ludic freedom diametrically opposed to the panopticism of Haussmann's boulevards, the street in all its iterations has become a privileged realm of microphysical surveillance, despite is persistent availability as a site of collective political resistance. Similarly, the control room (and the corporate–state apparatus to which it is appended) is not merely an a priori of despotic power; it is, like the empty tower at the center of Jeremy Bentham's panopticon, a vacuum with theological antecedents that is subject to a demystification as thorough as that accomplished by Zarathustra and his mountain.

About fifty years passed before interpreters of modern architecture—such as the architectural historian Manfredo Tafuri and his colleagues in Venice, most notably the philosopher Massimo Cacciari—had internalized the Simmelian/Weberian analysis of the modern metropolis. By then, however, that very sociological tradition had been transformed, particularly in the North American academy, into the systems sociology associated with Talcott Parsons or, later in Germany, with Niklaus Luhmann. In an untimely exchange, Tafuri's and Cacciari's trenchant decodings of the metropolis by way of the modernist avant-gardes were thus made possible by an earlier sociology of the city that was in the process of being absorbed into the same systems model from which the Italians recoiled in the architecture, city planning, and politics of their own time.

Much was learned from these decodings accomplished in the 1970s, which concentrated on the fundamental negativity of metropolitan experience and, hence, on the helplessness of the revolutionary or reformist avant-gardes facing the full force of capitalist development, which architecture was only ever able to reproduce mimetically. Nevertheless, their historical field of vision was restricted to the northern transatlantic, and they did little to account for the pulsating, dynamic globe that echoes through the ambiguous term "globalization." In the hands of someone like Fuller, who remains an anomaly for many historians but whose eccentricities are paradigmatic rather than exceptional, this globe was a system of systems to be designed and managed. In that sense, the geodesic dome and its underlying databases are to the "global" or "mega-" city what the arcades, street signs, and curios were to the modern metropolis. Not only because Fuller's dome optimized the mass production techniques that Benjamin, reading the architectural historian Sigfried Giedion, saw in the iron and glass enclosures of his *Passagen*. And not only because the geodesic dome, as an air-conditioned space frame built (more often than not) for the military–industrial complex, represented the purest, most Platonic instance of the airy claustrophobia sublimated into the glass-enclosed corporate lobby. But also because Fuller's dome was, first and foremost, an object of the architectural and urban imaginary projected at the scale of the planet and realized in the great cosmological tradition of Western dome-building since the Renaissance, an object at once entirely rational and entirely magical.

Understood as media, such objects reveal the dynamics of a world that otherwise appears exterior to them. In them, we confront what seems like a different set of problems, posed from a set of vantage points different from those that confronted early twentieth-century metropolitan thought. Still, to learn from that thought is to learn to see the control room as though it were the street, and vice versa. Aesthetic analysis can accomplish this, but only if it updates the tool kits inherited from the European avant-gardes and their philosophers, which were still linked (negatively, for the most part) to classical mimesis. In these tool kits was and remains the device, and the phenomenon, known as "abstraction." Abstraction was modern architecture's anti-mimetic answer to circulatory capital, wherein the supposed lifelessness of the commodity form was given an aesthetic language of its own. Its most fitting representative was not the German *Werkbund* or even the Bauhaus, but the Bauhaus Corporation (Bauhaus GmbH), which was set up in 1925 to enable the circulation of the lamps, household fittings, and furniture prototyped at the legendary design school. Alongside this in the urban realm stand the *Siedlungen,* or functionalist, middle-class housing estates built outside of Berlin and Frankfurt during that same period to train a multitude of Simmelian strangers in the protocols of mechanized domesticity.

Underlying this narrative is the premise that capital, fully formed, shapes or provokes a reaction in the sphere of art, or in culture more generally. Intuitively attractive as this premise may be, it excludes or at least downplays the possibility, evoked in the margins by Simmel and others, that aesthetic life partially *constitutes* (rather than simply derives from) economic life. To elaborate this possibility, we need first to understand more specifically what we mean by abstraction. Further, we need to ask: How, if at all, does abstraction continue to operate *aesthetically* in today's cities—and not only in those architectural artworks characterized by a degree of self-consciousness unavailable in the urban scene more generally? Is this simply a question of progressive, sequential development whereby the synchronized, geometrical "mass ornament" that Siegfried Kracauer found in Weimar-era spectacles and the factories that supported them is now to be found in the repetitive hum of business in Shanghai, with the *Siedlungen* replaced, in the imagination and on the ground, by the hundreds of cities by which the urbanization of the Chinese countryside is now being accomplished? To be sure, insight can be gained from such a transposition. However, not only does its developmentalist narrative (from Berlin to Shanghai) leave too many symptomatic assumptions intact; it fails to recognize the historicity of abstraction and indeed, of capital itself, along with associated concepts like reification and objectification, disenchantment and reenchantment, or alienation and estrangement.

Alternatively, we could collect a set of worldwide cultural "equivalents" to circulatory, global capital and its many outgrowths and mutations, in a manner similar to what Fredric Jameson has done with his Benjaminian reading of the Westin Bonaventure Hotel in Los Angeles.[1] Still, though Jameson offers many clues, we would not yet have fully approached a central transformation in the history of modern (and modernist) abstraction—that is, that the relation between part and whole, building and city, culture and capitalism, figured unconsciously in the arcades and semiconsciously in the *Siedlungen*, has become an apparent non-relation. It has, in other words, become *abstract* rather than merely contradictory or delinked. The aqueous dreamworlds of the modern, European metropolis, in which the outlines of an entire epoch could be discerned, have not simply been frozen into the opaque mirror worlds of postmodernity, poignantly captured in the self-referential corporate hotel. Rather, as Jameson suggests but does not fully develop, they have been displaced onto a different plane. So we cannot be content to compare the hotel lobbies of Pudong circa 2010 to the hotel lobbies of Berlin circa 1930. Instead, we must read urban artifacts not only as tangible, material evidence of the abstraction of modern life generated in the economic sphere, but also as abstraction itself.

Take Mumbai. In many ways this city epitomizes the workings of globalization's "financial imaginaries," which we can think of as a modification of what Simmel called the *Geistesleben*, or "mental life," of the modern metropolis. Financial imaginaries are sociocultural constructions through which circulate other sociocultural constructions, like "money," "credit," and "trust." All imaginaries belong to the realm of social practice, and my use of the term relies on its development in the work of a variety of thinkers, including Cornelius Castoriadis, Benedict Anderson, Arjun Appadurai, and Charles Taylor. Taylor, for one, has emphasized the practical dimensions of what he calls "modern social imaginaries" in making sense of social institutions in a way that enables these institutions to work. The "economy" is one such institution. More radically, Castoriadis speaks of "the imaginary institution of society" itself, as well as, reciprocally, the socially produced "instituting imaginaries" that, in effect, bring into being (generally oppressive) institutional forms out of an inchoate pre-societal "magma."[2]

But we must be clear about what we mean when we expand the notion of social imaginaries—all of those everyday ways in which a society imagines itself as a society—in the direction of cultural or aesthetic practices. Like social practices, cultural practices help to define what we mean when we speak, for example, of financialization. Finance capital courses through skyscrapers and slums alike; its presence or absence defines these physical forms but is also defined by them. As the raw material out of which what Appadurai has called "financescapes" are made, finance capital is much more, but also (by virtue of its abstraction) much less, than the sum total of the material goods and services in which it ostensibly trades; it is, strictly speaking, imaginary, though in a very real and practical sense rather than in the sense of a mere ideological illusion. As a calculatedly abstract relation among signs, value, and material things, finance capital circulates differently in Mumbai, New York, or São Paulo, constructing relationships among cities while assimilating each city's relative uniqueness and the different conflicts and communities that each city harbors. In this and other respects, architecture and urbanism form one element in a complex network of cultural practices that not only make financial globalization visible but also help bring it into being in the first place. This is because the imaginary construction and circulation of cultural meaning through material artifacts is a primary characteristic of political–economic processes, rather than a secondary effect.

In this give and take, site-specific particulars constantly trade places with general, axiomatic properties in a process that can best be described philosophically. Here I again refer to Simmel, and in particular to Simmel's canonical 1903 essay "The Metropolis and Mental Life," which extrapolates out of the empirical qualities of early twentieth-century European metropolitan life a set of general principles. These qualities include permanent restlessness, nervous energy, mechanical movement, and a heightened sense of abstraction associated with the money economy. For Simmel, these elicit an archetypal psychological reaction on the part of the metropolitan subject—what he calls a "blasé attitude." In an equally important essay of 1908, Simmel designated as the bearer of this attitude "the stranger," a prototypical urban figure who "comes today and stays tomorrow" without ever really settling down or fitting in.[8]

The arguments in these essays are based on Simmel's magnum opus of 1900, *The Philosophy of Money*. There, he argued that abstract monetary exchange associated with industrial capitalism found its social basis in a prevailing objectification of everyday urban experience that reflected what he called "the calculating character of modern times."[4] We need only recall the penetration of real estate development schemes into allegedly premodern crevices of urban space, such as slums or favelas, to recognize the continued relevance of this observation. But to understand its implications, we must look more closely at those ciphers in which appears the logic or syntax of finance, which we can provisionally describe as the syntax of credit. Because, far more than in Simmel's time, during the recent phase of accelerated growth, relationships among architecture and credit have structured our understanding of the contemporary city.

In New York as elsewhere, one result of this restructuring has been the elevation of the private real estate developer to near-mythic status, as occurred in the wake of 9/11 with the intense media attention lavished on the World Trade Center's developer–owner, Larry Silverstein. And, as occurred with the subsequent architectural competition for the redesign of the World Trade Center site, this fetishizing of the developer has been accompanied by a comparable elevation of the architect to celebrity status, especially in the case of the "signature architects" who now populate the international scene. Generally, the relationship between these two phenomena is poorly understood: the rise of the developer and the rise of the signature architect go hand-in-glove, but not only in the sense of each securing access to capital or prestige for the other. Much more significant, the rise of these two icons has to do with a *religiosity* that architecture and money still share. This affinity is based on a common language of "faith," which, as distinct from any historical religion, is addressed directly to economic abstractions and hence is as universal as the money form. To the extent that financial relations are ultimately relations of faith, in the sense of "faith" in higher forces such as the self-regulating, autopoietic financial markets that seem to lie outside of human control but are nevertheless constructed as benevolent, this language acquires the force of law.

In a city like Mumbai, which has witnessed an intense privatization of its physical infrastructures as well as of its civic discourse, tacit declarations of faith also furnish a legal or juridical imaginary for urban policy. Privatization policies largely imagine cities in terms of naturalized cycles of growth, much like living organisms. This correlates with the supposed laws driving local, regional, and interregional economies toward unlimited (and typically, under-regulated) expansion. Thus also, the competition between both developers and architects in different cities to build the tallest building in the world is not merely a question of egotism; it is the logical, symbolic fulfillment of the organicist myth of unlimited growth: the tallest tree in the unsustainable forests of expansionist capital.

So far, then, we have the idea of a quasi-religious faith in the markets, accompanied by an economic organicism—the supposedly natural law of unregulated, competitive expansion. But the crux of Simmel's philosophy of money lies in the interplay between abstraction and objectification. In his account, money is by turns a floating signifier *and* a concrete social (and technical) form. In that sense, we can adapt Marx's language and call money a *concrete abstraction*. Disregarding Simmel's tendency to resolve prematurely the contradictions that are laid bare by his own work, this notion is of particular relevance to his description of persons engaged in an exchange of *credit*. Simmel describes such persons as united in what he calls a "new, more abstract and comprehensive synthesis."[5] This synthesis is counterintuitively defined by increased distance as well as increased proximity. Rather than exchanging goods or even cash, people here exchange credit. As a result, they must trust one another more intimately than if they had exchanged more tangible things. Simmel explains, "In credit transactions the immediacy of value exchange is replaced by a distance whose poles are held together by trust in the same way as religiosity is more intense the greater the distance . . . between God and the individual soul in order to call forth the most considerable degree of *belief* so as to bridge the distance between them."[6]

Thus, the more abstract markets are—the more difficulty we have, say, in understanding today's credit markets—the more they require emotions like trust, belief, and quasi-religious faith to function. Moreover, just as the concrete abstractions of the money economy allowed Simmel a window onto the inner, psychic life of the modern, metropolitan subject, so too do urban artifacts, analyzed in a particular way, offer a window onto the psychic life of the postmodern, post-metropolitan city dweller, a psychic life that has now moved largely *outside*, into the light of day.

Although those who live in what Mike Davis has called the "planet of slums" might seem relatively indifferent to the mathematical abstractions on which this economy is built, they, too, are subject to these abstractions psychically, and not merely as depersonalized quanta.[7] Take, as an example, the Slum Redevelopment Authority (SRA) in Mumbai, which oversees the implementation of so-called Slum Rehabilitation Schemes (SRS) such as the one proposed for Dharavi, one of Asia's largest slums. Land is under intense pressure in Mumbai from real estate development; in response, governmental efforts like the SRA have sought to incentivize the private sector to "solve" a massive urban housing crisis by releasing valuable land for speculation.

By law, the SRA treats every slum structure existing prior to January 1, 1995, as a protected structure, and every inhabitant of such a structure is eligible for what is called "rehabilitation."[8] In a typical Slum Rehabilitation Scheme, the developer is effectively "hired" by the slum dwellers so that he may legally exploit them by treating their claim to housing as a form of property that can be exchanged, rather than as a political right to be administered by the state. In return for replacing every eligible slum structure with a bare minimum tenement unit (a material improvement on the existing shanties, to be sure), the developer gets development rights on what normally amounts to 50 percent of the land occupied by the slum. Such deals are made, with much political gamesmanship and bullying, simply because Mumbai's real estate market has made them quite profitable and is likely to continue to do so for the foreseeable future.

In addition to contriving to make it seem as though the market simply takes over from the state in providing for the basic needs of the population (which even developers admit is impossible for the city as a whole), this scheme does not so much resolve the underlying class conflict as abstract it into law. A vivid instance of this is found in a complex like the Imperial, a pair of luxury high-rise residential towers designed by the architect Hafeez Contractor on a slum-rehabilitation site in Mumbai's Tardeo neighborhood. This is not a particularly accomplished work of architecture. For Contractor, architecture is a game that is played to win rather than a refined art form. In this case, the game involved making the SRA legislation work on the site by balancing the socioeconomic demands of the luxury real estate market against the political demands of slum dwellers. The result is a monumental fissure running through the site that divides the very wealthy in the towers above from the very poor in the tenements below. The architecture of the complex, which consists mainly of overwrought, neo–Art Deco ornamentation above and functionalist regimentation below, is used simultaneously to produce and to cover up this fissure. More important, despite the domineering posture of the project's twin towers, their architecture and that of the "rehabilitated" slum over which they hover stand starkly separated from one another not only for their contrast of garish to humble but for the contrast between one architecture (that of the towers) that attempts to communicate and another architecture (that of the tenements) that does not.

This could be conventionally described as a contrast of figurative to abstract. More accurate would be to describe the project's stark, built-in divide as a concrete abstraction of another sort—a higher level of abstraction comparable to the abstractions of credit. Credit is built around trust, belief, and a quasi-religious faith—in the case of this project and of the SRA legislation in general, the faith that the real estate market will resolve the city's housing crisis, or, failing that, that it will allay the sense of crisis by rendering its fault lines ineffable. Here, the movement from use value to exchange value is turned on its head. Exchange value, in the form of luxury real estate, is made to seem capable of yielding surplus use value, in the form of the utilitarian tenements. This inversion, which is the principle according to which many "public–private" partnerships work, naturalizes the political–economic proposition underlying the SRA legislation by repositioning the slum dwellers (and, by extension, the public at large) as beneficiaries from whom the markets and their representatives ask only trust and faith. Enabled by the state, the market thus takes over as the biopolitical agent par excellence, and the slum dwellers are caught in a double bind of paternalism and primitive accumulation. In terms of urban realpolitik, they are also pitted against one another and forced to engage in Faustian bargaining for additional square feet based on the leverage acquired by holding out. Thus the Slum Rehabilitation Scheme *taken as a whole* can be described as a fetish: a quasi-religious object with seemingly magical powers that, like Fuller's equally metaphysical domes, is the product of rational calculation rather than its opposite.

But what does it mean to understand the ensuing relationship between architecture and capital not only as abstract, but also as *religious*? This question moves the analytic frame well beyond patronage (the developer as client) or analogy (that, say, the virtuality of contemporary architecture mimics the virtuality of contemporary finance), though both of these are factors. Nor is it simply that architecture as an art form is now considered a profitable amenity, along the lines of a model that was arguably invented in the 1980s in Houston by the developer Gerald Hines in collaboration with Philip Johnson. More than just a useful object turned fetish in the earlier Marxian sense, as a fragment of the financialized city the Imperial is an epistemic thing, a piece of the system in which the system's cognitive infrastructure, its way of making sense, is visible. It brazenly pits top against bottom, but in doing so, it warmly solicits trust and faith, delivering sense or meaning as a promissory note in the form of its central feature, the theological fissure that divides wealth from poverty. In unison with finance capital, this metonymic fragment of the city, like the city as a whole, promises abstractly to *mean something*—anything.

This promise is the other side of capital's demand for distracted attention that is met by straightforward commodity fetishism. More than Simmel or Weber (and closer to Marx), Benjamin and Kracauer were able to see that commodification entailed not only a process of *disenchantment* (i.e., of abstraction and of objectification) but also a process of *reenchantment*. Thus Benjamin's fascination with the dreamworlds harbored by the shopping arcades, which could properly be described as temples of commodities that anticipated the newer, more mythic, and more visibly enchanted department stores themselves. But if the combination of these two earlier building types—the department store and the arcade—would eventually yield the shopping mall, it is questionable whether malls carry the same sense of enchantment for today's shoppers. Instead, in another turn in the cycle of disenchantment and reenchantment, these have given way to representations of sheer quantity, sheer enumeration, as in the big-box megastores strewn across the suburban United States and well beyond. These spaces, like the mathematical and statistical techniques that structure many academic attempts to analyze the urban phenomena to which they belong, harbor a concealed aesthetic dimension that is central to neoliberal capitalism. Together with the general fascination with all things gigantic or "global," this dimension again gives rise to something like the Kantian mathematical sublime.[9]

Recall that for Kant, beautiful things are finite and therefore can be framed and represented. By contrast, the sublime is infinite and by definition, *unrepresentable*. This does not mean that it is inconceivable. On the contrary, Kant goes to some length to distinguish between the powers of the senses and the powers of the mind, arguing that the sublime is ultimately a form of thought wherein only the subjective response to an object, and not the object itself, can be properly termed "sublime." As an experience it is threatening, for example, when we are presented with the overwhelming force of nature in a turbulent storm, because this force cannot be fully captured in a finite representation. But precisely this threat to the senses—and in some cases, to human reason—gives the sublime its special status, yielding a distinctly mental form of comprehension that can intuit but not quite represent to itself (or picture) the phenomenon. The result is, in Kant's words, that "the object is apprehended as sublime [and not merely beautiful] with a pleasure that is possible only by means of a displeasure."[10]

This economy of pleasure and pain deriving from an encounter with natural force (or "might") is typically associated with what Kant calls the dynamically sublime, which elicits "the courage [to believe] that we could be a match for nature's seeming omnipotence."[11] Like natural landscapes, cities can harbor or elicit a sublime economy of pleasure and pain that differs qualitatively from a mimetic economy of resemblance. But more and more, they do so quantitatively, or, in Kant's terms, mathematically, as units or moments in an iterative series that extends toward the infinite. The consequent sense of mastery that, for example, is experienced paradoxically as quasi-religious faith in the rational basis of markets, derives from "supersensible" reason rather than from physical force: "*Sublime* [in the mathematical sense] *is what even to be able to think proves that the mind has a power surpassing any standard of sense*."[12]

Recognizing the difference allows us to grasp more fully the ways in which "faith" in abstraction constitutes urban real estate and other financial instruments and markets. These markets are not simply conduits, channels for the circulation of mathematical objects like mortgage-backed securities or derivatives. They are themselves abstract. Like the "globe" itself, real estate and other financial markets are imagined at some level to lie *outside representation*, but in the non-figural sense of an iterative series (Deleuze and Guattari's "thousand plateaus") tending toward infinite ramification. For, where Kant's media were the telescope and the microscope, which yielded the linear, scalar series by which he explains the mathematical sublime, ours is the computer, which yields the nonlinearities of feedback and of parametric, data-driven financial "networks."[18]

Correspondingly, like a nineteenth-century landscape painting that tries to capture the vastness of nature, architecture produced by and for the real estate markets presents to its many constituents a branching, indefinitely extended calculus performed by a system of systems so vast and encompassing—and ultimately, so threatening—that it has become sublimely pleasurable to contemplate it. Operating that system, at one end of its spectrum sit manifestly debased efforts like Contractor's Imperial Towers, while at the other end sit more self-consciously poetic ones, like Frank Gehry's IAC Building in New York's Chelsea neighborhood, or his "New York by Gehry" luxury residential tower in the city's Financial District. At both ends and across its span, this spectacle—which is the spectacle of the contemporary city proper, whether we are speaking of New York or Mumbai—brings a sense of awe but also, if Kant is right, mastery.[14]

Even in its most desultory forms, architecture mediates the socio–aesthetic life of cities to produce this combination of awe and mastery. In this, it shares with money, converted into the social relations of credit, a structural absence of meaning. Rather than affirming this absence, however, architecture today—that is, all buildings so designated—promises meaning through sublime abstraction, by bringing a global calculus to the street. On a sliding scale of conventional artistic merit, this promise recapitulates a counterthesis to Benjamin's notion of the aura's decline. Contrary to the expectation that commodification, mass production, and circulatory abstraction empty out cultural meaning into a disenchanted mirror play of surface effects, aura tends to increase in direct proportion to abstraction. As Simmel's "calculating character of modern times" approaches the mathematical, or more properly, the statistical sublime of the credit economy, meaning is permanently promised but also—a general law of circulation—permanently deferred, in an ineluctable dialectic of awe and mastery. By briefly sketching the outlines of such a dialectic, I hope to have given the impression that an aesthetic philosophy of the city is not only possible but required, in order to comprehend the transformations undergone by capital from one end of the century to the other.

Notes

1. Fredric Jameson, "Postmodernism; or, The Cultural Logic of Late Capitalism," *New Left Review* 146 (July–August 1984): 53–92, as well as *Postmodernism; or, The Cultural Logic of Late Capitalism* (Durham: Duke University Press, 1991), as well as "The Brick and the Balloon: Architecture, Idealism, and Land Speculation," and "Culture and Finance Capital," in *The Cultural Turn: Selected Writings on the Postmodern, 1983–1998* (London: Verso, 1998), 162–89, 136–61.

2. Charles Taylor, *Modern Social Imaginaries* (Durham: Duke University Press, 2004), 23–30, 69–82; Andreas Huyssen, ed., *Other Cities, Other Worlds: Urban Imaginaries in a Globalizing Age* (Durham: Duke University Press, 2008), introduction; Cornelius Castoriadis, *The Imaginary Institution of Society,* trans. Kathleen Blamey (New York: Polity Press, 1987).

3. Georg Simmel, "The Metropolis and Mental Life" and "The Stranger," in *The Sociology of Georg Simmel,* ed. and trans. Kurt H. Wolff (New York: Free Press, 1950), 409–424, 402–408.

4. Georg Simmel, *The Philosophy of Money,* ed. David Frisby, trans. Tom Bottomore and David Frisby, 2nd ed. (London: Routledge, 1990), 443.

5. Ibid., 480.

6. Ibid.

7. Mike Davis, *Planet of Slums* (New York: Verso, 2006). See also Arjun Appadurai, "Spectral Housing and Urban Cleansing: Notes on Millennial Mumbai," *Public Culture* 12, no. 3 (2000): 627–51.

8. For policy details on SRS overseen by Mumbai's SRA, see http://www.sra.gov.in/pgeSalientFeatures.aspx.

9. Kant, *Critique of Judgment,* 98, 103.

10. Ibid., 117.

11. Ibid., 120.

12. Ibid., 106.

13. On Kant's debt to other optical media (phantasmagoria) see Stefan Andriopoulos, *Ghostly Apparitions: German Idealism, the Gothic Novel, and Optical Media* (New York: Zone Books, 2013).

14. On Gehry, see the earlier version of this essay, "Financial Imaginaries: Toward a Philosophy of the City," *Grey Room* 42 (Winter 2011): 60–79.

3

The Thing about Cities

Is a city a thing? It may very well be that today, a city is first a piece of land subdivided into properties on which buildings are erected, to be bought and sold with the help of banks and other information processing, storage, and retrieval mechanisms. It may also be, then, that a city is no more than the sum total of those structures, the humans and nonhumans inside them, and the calculations that support them. To be sure, a city is also a social condenser, an infrastructural machine, and a congeries of symbols. But it still seems that now more than ever, the social "production of space" (in Henri Lefebvre's terminology) is imprisoned within the iron cage of real estate development: the city as calculation, number, ratio.

It is well-known that the metaphor of the capitalist "iron cage" is an artifact of translation originating with Talcott Parsons, the American sociologist who, in 1930, undertook the first translation into English of Max Weber's 1905 book *Die protestantische Ethik und der "Geist" des Kapitalismus* (*The Protestant Ethic and the Spirit of Capitalism*). In the Parsons translation, Weber cautions that, as Calvinist devotion to a vocational calling becomes the basis of the "modern economic order," humanity risks enclosure in an "iron cage" (*stahlhartes Gehäuse*).[1] Unlike Weber, Parsons was apparently unconcerned with the technical difference between iron (*Eisen*) and steel (*Stahl*), and so chose "iron cage" over the more literal rendering of "steel shell" (or more literally still, in a new translation, "shell as hard as steel").[2] Such technical differences notwithstanding, when one thinks about the wrought iron or factory-rolled steel frames that supported large, stone-clad monuments such as the Reichstag building (1894) or the Wertheim department store (1896) in Berlin, it is possible to imagine how, by 1905, European capitals threatened to become rigid cages of bureaucracy and calculation. But even then, Parsons's choice is somewhat anachronistic, especially since Weber's comment was clearly anticipatory, in that he expressed concern that this new order will persist "until the day that the last ton of fossil fuel has been consumed."[3]

Ambiguities regarding iron and steel abound during this period. Two years after Weber's essay, in 1907, a posthumous book by the German architect Alfred Meyer appeared under the title *Eisenbauten, ihre Geschichte und Æsthetik* (*Iron Construction: Its History and Aesthetic*), in which Meyer reviewed the achievements of nineteenth-century engineering in metal frame construction. Meyer did not systematically differentiate wrought iron from the increasingly ubiquitous "mild steel" alloy fabricated with the Bessemer process after 1858 or, via a Franco–Prussian business arrangement, the Siemens–Martin process after 1865. His book was followed by Sigfried Giedion's *Bauen in Frankreich, Eisen, Eisenbeton* (*Building in France: Iron, Ferro-Concrete*, 1928), which singled out the achievements of nineteenth-century French engineering, including (as did Meyer) the Eiffel Tower and the Galerie des Machines, both of which were built from rolled steel sections for the Paris Exposition of 1889. In one dossier of notes for his *Passagenwerk* (*Arcades Project*, 1927–40), titled "Iron Construction," Walter Benjamin makes frequent reference to Meyer and especially to Giedion. Gathered under the epigraph from Jules Michelet, "Each epoch dreams the one to follow," Benjamin's notes hint (without saying outright) that the iron and glass enclosures of the early nineteenth-century arcades, and the techno–social imaginaries to which they belonged, prefigured the much vaster, much more refined industrial complexes that were consolidated in the German war economy during the twentieth century's second decade, under nineteenth-century names such as Thyssen and Krupp.[4] Put differently, iron dreams steel.

With steel also come shells and other prosthetic enhancements of human capacity such as automobiles, the mass production of which was accelerated by what the German writer Ernst Jünger called the "total mobilization" of the First World War. In *Storm of Steel* (*In Stahlgewittern*), Jünger exclaimed that after the Battle of the Somme, "the German soldier wore the steel helmet, and in his features there were chiseled the lines of an energy stretched to the utmost pitch, lines that future generations will perhaps find as fascinating and imposing as those of many heads of classical or Renaissance times."[5] In a 1930 review of a collection of essays Jünger had edited under the title *Krieg und Krieger* (*War and War-*

rior), Benjamin responded sarcastically that in Jünger's glorified battle-field landscapes "every shell crater had become a problem, every wire entanglement an antinomy, every barb a definition, every explosion a thesis; by day the sky was the cosmic interior of the steel helmet, and at night the moral law above," which Benjamin saw as a perverse "upsurge" of the "German feeling for nature."[6] This is the other, organicist side of Weber's steel shell: the libidinal economy of war, etched into the "chis-eled" lines of its machines, in which was encased the cosmic remainder of the "Protestant ethic."

With the Great War, the technocratic calling had become a call to arms on both sides of the Atlantic and at the colonial extremities of the European empires. In its midst were cities. Berlin, where Benjamin, Jünger, and Weber all lived at different times, was on the periphery of the actual war but at the center of its buildup, its management, and its aftermath. This was the Berlin, for example, of Peter Behrens's Allge-meine Elektricitäts-Gesellschaft (AEG) turbine factory (1909), located in the working-class district of Moabit, where a demonstrative steel frame with neoclassical proportions rose above an expansive shop floor on which giant steel turbines for electric generators were assembled. A num-ber of AEG's other factories, which Behrens also designed and which became equally important for "total mobilization," were located nearby in "Red" Wedding. In 1914, AEG heir Walther Rathenau was put in charge of organizing and distributing raw materials for German war production, including iron ore and steel alloy from the Ruhr Valley for use in arma-ments, shells, helmets, and, increasingly after the war, buildings.

Other, less conspicuous hardware of metropolitan life was made of steel as well. In Weber's day, for example, a concierge was frequently to be found regulating the use of keys in the city's bourgeois neighborhoods, through probably less so in working-class Moabit or Wedding. By 1912, an imaginative Prussian locksmith had begun making a special kind of key that, as Bruno Latour has shown, modified social relations among apart-ment dwellers and concierges.[7] This so-called Berlin key, which could very well have been made from material that originated in the Krupp or Thyssen steelworks, had two heads fitted to a curious, two-position lock. One turn opens the door and allows the key to be pushed through the keyhole (rather than removed) upon entry, compelling a second turn, which locks the door before allowing the key to be withdrawn and the inhabitant to proceed on his or her way. The concierge, in possession of a special master key, could turn this mechanism "off" during the day, allowing the door to remain open and inhabitants and visitors to pass in and out under her watchful eye. Hence, as Latour says, the key fabricates in steel the social relations otherwise contained in the command: "Please bolt the door behind you during the night and never during the day."[8]

It has been said that the Berlin key, if not Berlin itself, is a "thing" and not an object. This reading, proposed by "thing theorist" Bill Brown, follows Latour in translating Martin Heidegger's philosophical category of "the thing" (*das Ding*) out of the premodern world of clay water jugs in which Heidegger finds it, and into the world of modern science and technology. Like the Berlin key, but unlike discrete objects that oppose themselves to discrete subjects, Heidegger's "things" act. They gather worlds around themselves. They socialize. They assemble. They differentiate as well as enfold humans and nonhumans. Indeed, things ultimately cancel the dialectic of subjects and objects, which, as Brown puts it, "has obscured patterns of circulation, transference, translation, and displacement."[9]

This view is obviously at odds with what Weber called objectification, or an exaggerated, "ideal" type of social and economic calculus that separates the world's elements into measurable units assembled out of inert materials such as iron or steel, which do no assembling and no socializing of their own. Weber's darker moments encourage us to see those Berlin technocrats locking and unlocking their doors with excessively rational keys as objects or automatons passing from one cage to another, condemned to the metallic life of a cog in the machine. Given the probability that many of its users left or entered their apartment lobbies on the way to or from office work or some other vocation that fit squarely into Weber's "new economic order" dominated by bureaucracy and rationalization, the Berlin key most likely did not unlock many iron cages or steel shells circa 1912. On the contrary, it secured them, and their class, race, and gender relations, even as it mediated all of these (as Latour points out) by allowing bourgeois officials to return home late from work and reliably lock the door behind them without waking the concierge.

Latour emphasizes that the "program of action" or "script" performed by the key ("Please bolt the door behind you during the night and never during the day") is milled in steel rather than set to words. In English, we might say that this property allows the Berlin key mechanism to carry two meanings of the term "hardware" at once: as a door lock and as an information processor. This puts it in some proximity to a more explicit account of the city itself—and possibly Berlin in particular—as a piece of hardware, sketched by the German media philosopher Friedrich Kittler in a brief, telegraphic essay written around the same time as Latour's.

Kittler describes the city as a "medium," by which he means a machine for processing, storing, and transmitting information—essentially, a large computer running population management software based on graph theory, addresses, and networks.[10] His sketch draws on Lewis Mumford's observation, in 1961, that "compared with the complex human order of the city, our present ingenious electronic mechanisms for storing and transmitting information are crude and limited."[11] It also recalls cybernetic urban planning techniques of the 1960s and 1970s such as those promulgated by the architect Christopher Alexander (whom Kittler also cites) or the MIT computer scientist Jay W. Forrester, in which architects and planners were effectively transformed into systems engineers. Absent Mumford's humanism, however, Kittler's description of the city, and especially the post–World War II European city, as a semiautonomous network of networks substantially limits human agency to a signal–response function, in the way that a traffic interchange orchestrates behavior along highly regulated infrastructural channels.

Kittler rightly sees in the postwar European city a megalopolitan tendency toward decentralization that displaces the symbolic and practical functions of the Hauptstadt, or capital city. Such decentralization, he argues, redistributes the city's central commands into a dispersed landscape of protocols embedded in interchanges and exchanges—"the wide green spaces and broad arteries of life in the Federal Republic," infrastructures that originate "from architectural plans during the World Wars to avert the next bomb terror."[12] Kittler's civil defense–oriented city-as-medium is therefore ultimately a sovereign network of switches, hubs, exchanges, memory banks, and input/output channels, circulating authorless commands that write end-of-history scripts. As he points out, the prototype for these commands is the "Hey, you there!" of Althusserian interpellation: the salutation of the state apparatus calling its subjects, converted into signs on the autobahns addressed to painted steel shells driving without destination.

In 1988, when his essay was first published, Kittler was teaching in Bochum. But the English translation, which appeared in 1996, is signed emphatically "Wilhelm von Humboldt University, Berlin," where he was teaching at the time, perhaps indicating the presence of that city between the essay's lines.[18] In addition to interrupting Berlin's transportation networks such as the U-Bahn and interchanges such as Potsdamer Platz, the Wall and its accompanying territorial arrangement cut off half the symbolic head of German sovereignty. Removed to Bonn, near the border with France, the West German Parliament settled for ad hoc architectural arrangements until 1987, when construction began on a new plenary chamber. On the eastern side of the Wall, the other half city's ongoing function as Hauptstadt was marked, in 1976, by a steel and mirrored glass parliament building, the Palast der Republik (Palace of the Republic), which doubled as a socialist civic center. After 1992, the new German parliament was housed in the plenary chamber in Bonn, an anti-monumental, filigreed steel and glass structure that all but shouted "Democracy!" Finally, in 1999, the governing body returned to Berlin and to the renovated Reichstag building, which had been duly equipped by the architect Norman Foster with its own filigreed steel and glass dome.

In calling elsewhere for a democratic "parliament of things," or a politics of material objects assembling and disassembling publics around themselves ("Dingpolitik"), Latour suggests that the nostalgic "imitation" of earlier parliaments in the renovated Reichstag "doesn't seem nearly enough to absorb the new masses that are entering political arenas."[14] Perhaps. But in this new glass and steel dome, Benjamin's arcades had returned to the scene of the crime. In place of the old panoramas, a surrealistic mirrored glass funnel on the inside of the dome and directly above the plenary chamber reflects, in the round, parliamentary activities below to visitors traversing the dome's spiral ramp above. Hence, on the outside of the democracy machine, steel, glass, and pseudo-transparency; on the inside, an inversion of the glass mirrors wrapping the Palast der Republik. Inevitably, as if to erase any material evidence of a subliminal east–west technology transfer, the former East German parliament was subsequently demolished. In its place were prepared the foundations for a solid new replica of the site's old Hohenzollern Palace (Stadtschloss) to rise out of the ruins of socialism: steel and mirrored glass now dreaming stone. To add tragedy to farce, the actual steel salvaged from the demolition of the Palast was melted down and sold to a Turkish manufacturer of structural components for use in Dubai in the construction of the Burj Khalifa luxury apartment tower.[15]

The problem lies, then, in the different ways in which we might construe things as mediators, and in the different social relations they store. With Latour and Kittler in the 1980s, we have Berlin as hardware in both senses of the term: figured in a key that shapes a city's social codes but does not unlock its cages, and as a half-decapitated bureaucratic information-processing machine. Where Kittler's tone is vaguely apocalyptic, Latour's is archaeological. If Kittler is correct, the new Reichstag dome is an anachronism beneath which lie the distributed networks of an informatic, managerial Eurozone built out of the rubble of the World Wars. If Latour is correct, the new dome is an irrelevant distraction from the urgent problem of assembling global publics at a moment when idealized representations of the globe—such as domes—have been rendered obsolete by the messiness of actually existing globalization. Both readings are plausible. The difference is that, for Kittler, media (or things) simply mediate, eventually writing humanistic interfaces like domes or parliaments out of the equation in a "total mobilization" without commandants, only commands; while for Latour, things mediate social relations and vice versa, proliferating hybrid networks of humans and nonhumans in which the pragmatic possibility of a negotiated peace remains on the table.

Neither type of mediation, however, fully explains the softening of the city's hard shell in the great urban experiment that was actually under way in West Berlin during the years these two texts were written: the Internationale Bauausstellung (International Building Exhibition, or IBA), begun in 1978 and formally concluded in 1987. Despite its international pretensions, the IBA, which was run as a quasi-public agency, entailed a largely municipal effort to adjust social housing policy and practice in West Berlin to the requirements of an uncertain real estate market while preserving some but not all of the protections and guarantees afforded by the postwar welfare state. Its ethos and its aesthetic program were self-consciously anti-technocratic, and were guided by the partnership, unanticipated by Weber, between capitalism and humanism that has come to characterize the neoliberal city. For the IBA's architects, who came from across Western Europe as well as from the United States, the mandate was "critical reconstruction," or the rebuilding of the traditional city fabric in an idiom sensitive to the scale and texture of nineteenth-century Berlin—Berlin, that is, before iron cages or steel shells, before "total mobilization," before the Third Reich, and before the Wall.

The IBA consisted of two sections: the New Buildings Section, in which were constructed numerous relatively low-cost, mixed-income apartment blocks, and the Careful Urban Renewal Section, in which existing social or subsidized housing was retrofitted and existing blocks completed. The retrofits and new construction in the Careful Urban Renewal Section tended to be built or overseen by local housing authorities, and involved organized resident input or other mechanisms intended to protect low-income, often immigrant residents from market-based speculation. In contrast, most of the new housing in the New Buildings Section was built by private real estate developers (under government subsidy) who had been selected through design competitions run by the IBA GmbH, the publicly funded corporate arm of the IBA, for each project site. Ultimately, the IBA comprised about 3,000 new apartments—"dwelling units" in English—and 5,500 renovated ones.[16]

The IBA New Buildings Section effectively converted parts of West Berlin like South Tiergarten and South Friedrichstadt, as well as the more peripheral Tegel, into open-air architecture museums exhibiting mostly gentle, anti-steel interpretations of the *Mietskaserne,* or traditional perimeter block, imposed by the IBA planners. Inside, the units largely followed formulas stipulated by the developers in consultation with the city's housing commission, reinforcing the grip of economic calculation on an everyday life that was mediated elsewhere (and earlier) by the Berlin key. While outside, the humanist "script" written by the façades was made more pronounced by their proximity to the Wall and to the regimented concrete *Plattenbauten* (prefabricated apartment blocks) on the other side, to which they formed an unambiguous rebuke.

In a similar vein, the English translation of Latour's essay includes a footnote that emphasizes its origins in pre-1989 West Berlin, "which," he says, "was at the time besieged by real socialism."[17] By this one assumes he meant the half city's isolation within the territory of East Germany and its relation to other kinds of iron cages (and curtains). But there are different "real socialisms," not all of which can be straightforwardly opposed, as idealist absolutisms, to the pragmatic, democratic assemblage of publics around bourgeois steel keys. And there are also real capitalisms that compel the erection of walls rather than their disassembly, thus furthering the militarization of the city in a not-so-distant echo of Jünger's "total mobilization."

For the latter see São Paulo, a "city of walls" pockmarked by segregated urban enclaves.[18] In the 1980s, when the paint on the IBA housing was still fresh, it became common for wealthy and upper-middle-class Paulistanos to enclose themselves in high-rise housing blocks surrounded by defensive walls. Armed guards often sat, and still sit, at the gates to these compounds. Like Berlin concierges from earlier days, these guards enact a social script written in steel that monitors the comings and goings of residents, their guests, and service workers from the favelas, the difference being that the mediating steel "things" are guns rather than keys. Soaring urban crime and vast income discrepancies associated with privatization and the economics of "structural adjustment" largely explain this state of affairs. But São Paulo's enclaves are anything but anomalous. They are at the far end of a new norm—the city as a collection of little Berlins, walled or gated enclosures that assemble and enfold entire worlds within, rather than around, themselves.

Correspondingly, not all the "real socialisms" stored in Berlin's hardware come from behind the iron curtain. In the early days of the IBA, the Portuguese architect Álvaro Siza Vieira designed a fragment of housing (in Kreuzberg, near the Schlesisches Tor U-Bahn station and adjacent to the Wall) that turned a corner and partially restored the continuity of a block that had been heavily damaged by Allied bombs. Shortly after the building was completed, an enigmatic, awkward graffito was anonymously scrawled across its crest: "Bonjour tristesse," "Hello sadness," quoted inexplicably from an Otto Preminger film based on a popular French novel. In that scrawl, as in the building itself, is a note of existential resignation. Both seem to indicate that, in West Berlin, the best one could do was to acknowledge the ruined, split polis with the reconstructed urban fragment. In Siza's hands, in a neighborhood heavily populated by working-class Turkish immigrants, this meant combining the stripped-down neoclassicism of Adolf Loos with the rationalist linear blocks, or *Zeilenbau*, associated with Ernst May: a Weberian architecture if there ever was one, softened and pried open by history.

But this modest, solemn piece of "critical reconstruction" also has another past. The setting is the Portuguese spring of 1974. It is a revolutionary moment at a time when revolution had been declared obsolete by the American standard-bearers of a postmodern, postindustrial society. A semigovernmental housing agency, SAAL (Servicio de Apoio Ambulatorio Local, or Ambulatory Local Support Service), was established by the socialist coalition that emerged after a leftist military coup overthrew the

Caetano dictatorship on April 25, 1974, in what is known as the Carnation Revolution. Under the auspices of SAAL, as in limited sections of the IBA (including Siza's project), neighborhood committees initiated a variety of self-managed social housing schemes, mainly in Oporto and Lisbon. Siza, as part of a "technical brigade" tasked with supporting the needs of resident committees in an often conflictual participatory process, designed two SAAL housing projects in Oporto, the Bouça and São Victor houses, both of which were completed in 1977.

Technically and architecturally, Siza's IBA housing project in Kreuzberg learns from and reproduces some of these results, as social–democratic capitalism sublimates socialist experimentation, and West Berlin silently but inexorably commemorates the Portuguese revolution. The translation was limited and mostly abortive; Siza eventually withdrew from designing the actual dwelling units.[19] Hence another possible meaning for the graffito, "Bonjour tristesse": an ominous command, like the grinning "Hey, you there!" of capital consolidating its post-steel partnership with the liberal state; but also an ambiguous, automated "Hello" from a thing that has only just awakened.

Like computers, things have memories. And if cities are things and not merely objects, that is because the memories they store do not all lead to the same place, as Andreas Huyssen has shown with special reference to Berlin.[20] Latour's coy aside about the dangers of "real socialism" notwithstanding, the city's memory banks indiscriminately store all histories, like a bureaucrat filing papers in a steel drawer, or backing up files on a hard drive or in the cloud. Some of these, like the memories recorded in Siza's building in Kreuzberg, do not follow the dominant script. Meanwhile, in Berlin as elsewhere, austere commands written in steel have been replaced by warm appellations—"Hey, you there!"—addressed to humans by gregarious machines. Among such machines is the swirling outdoor atrium just off the reconstructed Potsdamer Platz—the new Reichstag's sociable, commercial companion and the city's last arcade, built under the sign of Sony and Daimler. Its post-historical cheerfulness is of a piece with the industrialization of memory in the fin de siècle, post–Cold War amnesia of memorials and museums, but also in the dwelling units that constitute the city's fabric. As calculation, number, ratio, those units record, impassively and with precision, the friendly march of the real estate developer—history's assassin—into the narrowest crevices of urban life. But they also impolitely remember other times and other places, possibly in the future, after "the last ton of fossil fuel has been consumed," when the soft shell of capitalist humanism is met by the greeting "Bonjour tristesse."[21]

Notes

1. Max Weber, *The Protestant Ethic and the Spirit of Capitalism*, trans. Talcott Parsons (1930; repr., New York: Charles Scribner's Sons, 1958), 181.

2. Max Weber, *The Protestant Ethic and the "Spirit" of Capitalism and Other Writings*, ed. and trans. Peter Baehr and Gordon C. Wells (New York: Penguin, 2002), 121. Baehr has provided a detailed analysis of the issues surrounding the translation of this figure in "The 'Iron Cage' and the 'Shell as Hard as Steel': Parsons, Weber, and the Stahlhartes Gehäuse Metaphor in The Protestant Ethic and the Spirit of Capitalism," *History and Theory* 40 (May 2001): 153–69.

3. Weber, *The Protestant Ethic and the "Spirit" of Capitalism and Other Writings*, 121.

4. Walter Benjamin, *The Arcades Project*, ed. Rolf Tiedemann, trans. Howard Eiland and Kevin McLaughlin (Cambridge: Belknap Press of Harvard University Press, 1999), "F: [Iron Construction]," 151–70. By the 1910s, Thyssen & Co. (originating in 1867) and Fried. Krupp AG (originating in 1811) were two of Germany's largest steelworks.

5. Ernst Jünger, *The Storm of Steel: From the Diary of a German Storm-Troop Officer on the Western Front* (New York: Howard Fertig, 1996), 109. In passing, translator Peter Baehr has distinguished Weber's use of "steel" figuratively, to denote passivity, from Jünger's more active sense, in "The 'Iron Cage' and the 'Shell as Hard as Steel,'" 164. In terms of the interdependence of bureaucracy and ("total") military mobilization, however, the distinction appears less firm.

6. Walter Benjamin, "Theories of German Fascism: On the Collection of Essays War and Warriors, Edited by Ernst Jünger" (1930), trans. Jerolf Witkoff, in *Walter Benjamin: Selected Writings Volume 2, 1927–1934*, ed. Michael W. Jennings, Howard Eiland, and Gary Smith (Cambridge, Belknap Press of Harvard University Press, 1999), 318–19.

7. Bruno Latour, "The Berlin Key; or, How to Do Words with Things," trans. Lydia Davis, in P. M. Graves-Brown, *Matter, Materiality and Modern Culture* (London: Routledge, 2000), 10–21. The earliest version of the article is "Inscrire dans la nature des choses ou la clef berlinoise," *Alliages* 6 (1991): 4–16.

8. Latour, "The Berlin Key," 17.

9. Bill Brown, "Thing Theory," *Critical Inquiry* 28, no. 1 (2001), 12. Heidegger's 1950

lecture "Das Ding" is available in Heidegger, *Poetry, Language, Thought*, trans. Albert Hofstadter (New York: Harper Perennial, 2001), 161–80.

10. Friedrich A. Kittler, "The City Is a Medium," trans. Matthew Griffin, *New Literary History* 27, no. 4 (1996): 717–29.

11. Lewis Mumford, *The City in History: Its Origins, Its Transformations, and Its Prospects* (New York: Harcourt, Brace & World, 1961), 569. The passage is quoted in Kittler, "The City Is a Medium," 721.

12. Kittler, "The City Is a Medium," 727.

13. Ibid. The original published version of the essay, which does not contain a reference to Berlin, can be found in Dietmar Steiner, Georg Schöllhammer, Gregor Eichinger, and Christian Knechtl, eds., *Geburt einer Hauptstadt am Horizont* [*The Birth of a Capital City on the Horizon*] (Vienna: Edition BuchQuadrat, 1988), 507–32.

14. Bruno Latour, "From Realpolitik to Dingpolitik; or, How to Make Things Public," in *Making Things Public: Atmospheres of Democracy*, ed. Latour and Weibel (Cambridge and Karlsruhe: MIT Press and ZKM/Center for Art and Media, 2005), 31.

15. Arno Maierbrugger, "Steel from Historic East German Palace Used to Build Burj Dubai," *Gulf News*, August 10, 2008, http://gulfnews.com/business/construction/steel-from-historic-east-german-palace-used-to-build-burj-dubai-1.124124. The name of the Burj Dubai (Dubai Tower) was later changed to Burj Khalifa, in tribute to Sheik Khalifa bin Zayed al-Nahayan, president of the United Arab Emirates and emir of Abu Dhabi, which provided bailout funds to ensure the project's completion.

16. A detailed account of the Internationale Bauausstellung is given in Wallis Miller, "IBA's 'Models for a City': Housing and the Image of Cold-War Berlin," *Journal of Architectural Education* 46, no. 4 (1993): 202–16.

17. Latour, "The Berlin Key," 21n2. The footnote does not appear in the 1991 French version.

18. See Teresa P. R. Caldeira, *City of Walls: Crime, Segregation, and Citizenship in São Paulo* (Berkeley: University of California Press, 2000); and Caldeira, "From Modernism to Neoliberalism in São Paulo: Reconfiguring the City and Its Citizens," in *Other Cities, Other Worlds: Urban Imaginaries in a Globalizing Age*, ed. Andreas Huyssen (Durham: Duke University Press, 2008), 51–77.

19. Stages in the design of the building are documented in Pier Luigi Nicolin, "Alvaro Siza: Three Projects for Kreuzberg," *Lotus International* 32 (1981): 44–59; in "Wohnbau in Berlin: Internationale Bauausstellung Berlin 1984," *Bauforum* 17, no. 104 (1984), 22; and in the construction drawings accompanying the reprinting of Nicolin's account in *Alvaro Siza: Poetic Profession* (Milan: Edizioni Electa, 1986), 145–59.

20. See especially the essays related to Berlin in Andreas Huyssen, *Twilight Memories: Marking Time in a Culture of Amnesia* (London: Routledge, 1995) and *Present Pasts:*

Urban Palimpsests and the Politics of Memory (Stanford: Stanford University Press, 2003). In "Time and Cultural Memory at Our Fin de Siècle," the introduction to *Twilight Memories,* Huyssen writes, "The difficulty in the current conjuncture is to think memory and amnesia together rather than simply to oppose them. . . . Memory is no longer primarily a vital and energizing antidote to capitalist reification via the commodity form, a rejection of the iron cage homogeneity of an earlier culture industry and its consumer markets. It rather represents the attempt to slow down information processing" (7). Or, we can add, to undo its deletions and restore its erasures.

21.   My thanks to Andreas Huyssen for his comments on an earlier version of this text.

4

Public and Common(s)

Two terms, or really, two groups of terms, seem today to gather competing ideas as to how anything like a collective, collectivity, or collective space might be conceived. The city figures prominently in both. On the one hand we have the set of concepts assembled around the term "public," as in public realm, public sphere, public space, public sector, and "the public" itself. On the other is the set of concepts associated with the term "common": the common(s), common sense, and common wealth. The latter set resonates with communism, communal, and the like. But neither should its usage by environmentalists to debate an oft-misunderstood "tragedy of the commons" be overlooked. Similarly, as the controversy over a potential "public option" in American health care reform showed, conventional Anglophone usage associates "public" with the welfare state and with liberal/progressive political reform more generally.

Circulating between these two sets is the category of the "social," as in socialism, but also as used by the philosopher Hannah Arendt to differentiate the modern managerial sphere, including both state- and market-based social or behavioral management, from the classical res publica. According to Arendt, modernity is characterized by the preponderance of managerial practices—"housekeeping," as she puts it—that have emerged from the classical domestic sphere, the *oikos*, to organize and dominate the life of the *polis*, or city. These practices take as their field of activity a newly constituted object—society—thereby blotting out the distinction between public and private life, or the distinction between household management and political life, on which city-states were founded in classical times. Many commentators have pointed out that, in accepting uncritically this division of labor, Arendt idealizes the Greek *polis*, in which only male citizens participated in "public" (i.e., political) life, with women and slaves confined to the household (the "private" realm, or *oikos*) and its internal, domestic economy.

For Arendt, the *polis* constitutes a "space of appearance," in which being-in-public, or "publicity," is effectively synonymous with politics. More than simply a public square or forum, the space of appearance is potentially ubiquitous. As she puts it, "appearance—something that is being seen and heard by others as well as by ourselves—constitutes reality,"[1] meaning that publics are formed only in the presence of others. In the sort of democratic city-state that Arendt has in mind, these others are equals, to whom fall the responsibilities of governance. Such governance is decidedly agonistic, in that "the reality of the public realm relies on the simultaneous presence of innumerable perspectives and aspects in which the common world presents itself."[2] This perspectivism renders Arendt's "public appearance" a kind of struggle among equals for the heart and soul of the *polis*, which is what differentiates it, for her, from the false "objectivity" of the money economy and of administrative rationality more generally.

In passing, Jürgen Habermas associates Arendt's "rise of the social" with the emergence of the bourgeois public sphere (*Öffentlichkeit*). This sphere is, again ideally, a social space in which transparent communication among equals occurs in such a manner that these individuals ("private persons," or *Privatmannen*) come together to form a public capable of laying claim on state politics. It is also, as Habermas says, the space where "public opinion" (*opinion publique*, or its analogue, *öffentliche Meinung*) is formed. Remembering the eighteenth-century pamphleteer Thomas Paine, we can add that it is also the space in which "common sense" is formed. Its principal matrix comprises the assembled instruments of civil society such as the press (or media), which accompany the "traffic in commodities and news" characteristic of European capitalism from its mercantilist phase onward. Hence Habermas's public is a bourgeois "reading public" who, in the late eighteenth century, frequented libraries, gathered in Berlin cafés to discuss matters of state, and published their opinions in daily broadsheets and in monthly political journals.[3]

Like Arendt's, Habermas's idealizations have been vigorously challenged, not least by feminist theorists who note the hidden exclusions, often determined by gender, by which the bourgeois public sphere is constituted. In one important response that is still in considerable sympathy with Habermas's project, Nancy Fraser has offered the category of "subaltern counterpublics" to throw off balance Habermas's implicitly male, white, moneyed, or otherwise hegemonic public sphere. By this Fraser means those groups or categories of citizens and noncitizens that are structurally excluded, usually by combinations of gender, race, and class, from the political commerce of bourgeois capitalism. Drawing on Gayatri Chakravorty Spivak's translation of the Gramscian "subaltern," or voiceless subject, for Marxist feminism, Fraser's "subaltern counterpublics" describes a whole host of potentially incommensurable public spheres, or "parallel discursive arenas where members of subordinated social groups invent and circulate counterdiscourses to formulate oppositional interpretations of their identities, interests, and needs."[4] Most critically, these spheres do not simply coexist in a homogeneous gel, a metapublic sphere or space in which their differences can be democratically adjudicated. Rather, they occupy a differentiated field of "stronger" and "weaker" powers, in which the very constitution of counterpublics subordinates them by definition to the pervasive force of bourgeois (i.e., masculinist) norms, thus marking what Fraser calls the "limits of actually existing democracy."

It is interesting that Arendt uses the section heading "The Public Realm: The Common" to distinguish this category from is private partner, which is subtitled "Property." In this second sense running alongside the sense of public as publicity, what is public is, for Arendt, outside the realm of property relations. It is, simply, "the world itself, insofar as it is common to all of us and distinguished from our privately owned place in it"[5]—whereupon the gradual, historical erasure of the sharp line dividing public interests from private ones also abolishes the sense of a common world, to be replaced with "mass society" comprising merely unrelated, juxtaposed fragments rather than actual or virtual publics, and capable of relating only at the level of economic exchange or its arithmetic equivalents.

It may seem odd, then, that Arendt begins *The Human Condition* (1958), the work in which she most comprehensively outlines her thesis, with the image of the Soviet Sputnik satellite, humankind's first instance of mechanized escape from earthly conditions, which was launched in 1957. For Arendt, Sputnik captures the whole modern travesty of enlightened pub-

lic knowledge ("science," as she calls it) enlisted to enact long-held philosophical and religious fantasies of otherworldly life. Likewise, this orbiting machine bears witness to what she understatedly calls the "uncom-
fortable" political circumstances of the Cold War.[6] But precisely as such,
Sputnik and its American counterpart, Explorer, were also products of
the medium of publicness that was the sine qua non for both (or all) sides
of the Cold War impasse: the modern state.

I pointedly describe the state as a "medium" to steer away from disputes
over statist versus non-statist political models that fetishize abstractions
in positive or negative terms, and toward an infrastructural, almost technological, conception of the state and its institutions. By this I do not
mean technocratic, but pragmatic—the state, or the "public sector," not
as an idealized or abstract entity, but as a historical constellation of institutions, practices, protocols, and material complexes. Sputnik and its
descendants are products of such infrastructures, a term that connotes,
in its commonest usage, a certain publicness in its own right. To put it
another way: Sputnik is unthinkable without the material infrastructures
of the state, as well as the imaginaries that circulate through those infrastructures, and the reflexive "apparatuses," or instruments of societal reg-
ulation, in which these two levels join, as described by thinkers like Louis
Althusser and Michel Foucault. Arendt is able to discern in Sputnik's orbit
a compelling metaphor for humanity's efforts to delink from that "space
of appearance"—Earth—to which public life is ultimately tethered. She
is less concerned, however, with the strange fact that the very invention—the modern state—that makes it all possible is presumed at both
ideological poles to represent whatever is left of her ideal public, as in a
distorting mirror.

Something like this is also at work in the Habermasian public sphere, as
well as in Fraser's counterpublics. In both, the state sits firmly in the background, as the locus of bourgeois political address percolating through
civil society, or as the ultimate site of contestation over rights, voice,
transparency, and equity first elaborated in counterpublic arenas. In that
sense, it is as though the term "public" shares a fate with the modern state
itself.

In their collaborative trilogy of *Empire* (2000), *Multitude* (2004), and
Commonwealth (2009), Michael Hardt and Antonio Negri take this proposition to its logical conclusion. They argue that during the course of the
twentieth century, the world order based on the sovereignty of nation-

states has been gradually and unevenly replaced by what they call "imperial sovereignty," or Empire, a transnational, biopolitical capitalism coursing fluidly through both affective and instrumental channels. For Hardt and Negri, then, the categories of "public" and "private," linked historically with state socialism or social democracy on the one hand, and liberal republicanism on the other, simply connote two different means to the same end: the reproduction of capital. Writing four decades after Sputnik, they follow many critics of Soviet-style socialism in suggesting that this system merely substituted a centralized state for a market oligarchy to manage industrial/capitalist production, and thus served as a prelude to the decentered sovereignty of neoliberal capital. To confront the latter, they propose a political philosophy that substitutes older categories like "the people" and "the state," or "private" and "public," with new ones, like "multitude" and "common wealth," or "singularity" and "common."

Key to this reconceptualization is the claim that the common is not merely a postindustrial upgrade of the modern state, which is historically linked with the rise of industrial capitalism. Hardt and Negri define this common most succinctly as: (1) the natural environment, its resources, and the products they yield; and (2) the products of social interaction, such as codes, languages, affects, information, and other forms of knowledge.[7] Especially in this second form, their sense of the common is wholly immanent to biopolitical practice: that is, a common wealth is constantly being produced and circulated in those everyday processes by which life itself is sustained, enhanced, articulated, or otherwise organized, in areas as diverse as manufacturing, health care, and housing on the one hand, and education, scientific research, and the arts on the other.

Hardt and Negri therefore encourage us to look "beyond public and private" for philosophical concepts and political practices capable of challenging and transforming the "republic of property" that underlies both categories. Most frequently, they find models in the insurgent, bottom-up politics of the counter- or alter-globalization movements that proliferated in the 1990s, or in the autonomous democracy practiced by groups such as the Mexican Zapatistas. They see the heterogeneous, sometimes fractious "multitude" that comes together in these and countless other, less visible movements as the contrary to the homogenized modern masses or an abstract, universal "public." But neither does it merely replace or multiply these. Instead, for Hardt and Negri, the multitude constitutes a novel historical subject that draws its energies from the constant production of common goods and especially common knowledge and services, provoked by resistance to capitalism but not wholly determined by it.

What are these goods and services? Hardt and Negri place a great deal of emphasis on the productivity of "immaterial labor," the type of labor characteristic of what is sometimes called the service sector. They have therefore been criticized for deemphasizing or ignoring manual labor and its accompanying subject, the working class. To this they argue that it is not a matter of one class or sector replacing another, but of one logic—applying to all classes and sectors—replacing, or at least displacing, another. Immaterial labor is based above all on communication, and it is this they seek to release in radically transformative, revolutionary directions. Think of Sputnik, then, as a triumph of immaterial labor held captive by the state.

Here, too, we can discern an etymological resonance—common(s), communication—that is sharpened when Hardt and Negri claim that "the common does not refer to traditional notions of either the community or the public; it is based on the *communication* among *singularities* and emerges through collaborative social processes of production."[8] (In their idiom, a singularity is more like a unique, internally divided and incalculable point, rather than an individual unit.) Elsewhere, they add one more term to the etymological chain, by arguing that "what the private is to capitalism and what the public is to socialism, the common is to communism."[9]

Hardt and Negri are quick to distinguish this communism from the state-based authoritarian socialisms to which that term became affixed during the course of the twentieth century. And if anything, many of their proposals for "a reformist program for capital" are distinctly neo-Keynesian: provide the physical, social, and educational infrastructure for biopolitical production; open the intellectual and cultural commons to all; establish "open citizenship" across borders; enhance economic freedom with a guaranteed income; build participatory democracy into all levels of government. For them, "saving" capitalism from its self-destructiveness in this way is not an end in itself, but the first stage of a transition that "requires the growing autonomy of the multitude from both private and public control; the metamorphosis of social subjects through education and training in cooperation, communication, and organizing social encounters; and thus a progressive accumulation of the common."[10]

Less clear, however, is the medium by which *communication* becomes *common*. Unlike many theorists of the communicative public sphere, Hardt and Negri have relatively little to say about the specific forms of mediation by which collective subjectivities are formed. By this I mean not only technological mediation, as in the properties of those communications systems by which a multitude comes into its heterogeneous being-in-common, but also other mediating instruments, like social structures (the family, the nation) or institutions (schools, hospitals, housing, workplaces, prisons, communications networks). If the segmented realm of public and private is to be replaced by the networked realm of the common, what will replace these mediators?

In this sense, Hardt and Negri's "common" is subject to criticisms analogous to those that have been leveled at Habermas's version of the public sphere. Not that it homogenizes otherwise heterogeneous subjectivities or submits them to the rule of an arbitrary norm; but rather, that in subsuming the dyad singularity/multiplicity into a common, nonhomogeneous substrate, it potentially underestimates the differentials, interferences, and asymmetries comprising that substrate's communicative infrastructures. From its beginnings, communications theory has emphasized the necessary loss of information in any communicational transaction. Hardt and Negri seem to assume that this loss is ultimately negligible, and that the interference and distortions that accompany all communication are superseded by the common wealth generated by cooperative labor among singular subjects. I do not wish to argue the contrary, that the inevitable mediations of intersubjective life render any common impossible from the start. Rather, I want to ask whether the exhausted category of the public, and with it, the ruined infrastructures of the state—including Sputnik's descendants—might be reappropriated as media, or fragmentary elements of a media system, in which life-in-common can take place.

At a political level as well as at a philosophical one, this means modulating the directness of direct or participatory democracy with a media theory of communications. Hardt and Negri suggest as much when they cite recent scholarship on radically democratic media practices. And by no means do they argue that the common emerges out of some primal, unmediated field of social and economic activity. But nowhere do they work through the structural, rather than circumstantial, particulars of the very mediating infrastructures they propose to "save" capitalism from itself while simultaneously preparing the ground for its multitudinous alternative.

Here is one example. Among the many sites in which they discern "specters of the common" is the contemporary metropolis, or really, the global city. One measure of the city as a site of biopolitical production appears in the vexing problem (for traditional Marxists) of ground rent. In urban economics, a labor theory of value has some difficulty in accounting for the intangibles of location, services, and other "quality of life" factors, which economists sometimes term "externalities." Hardt and Negri point out that these seeming externalities actually register "the general social circuits of biopolitical production and reproduction of the city," which are subject to reappropriation.[11] Another way of saying this is that the city mediates value production through its material infrastructures. Among other things, these infrastructures typically support transportation, communication, education, security, health, housing, and commerce, and are variously associated with the state, the private sector, or both.

Elsewhere, referring to the metropolis as the "inorganic body of the multitude," Hardt and Negri suggestively argue that *the metropolis is to the multitude what the factory was to the industrial city*," in three ways.[12] First, in that the contemporary city is "the space of the common," a privileged site in which an "artificial common" of "languages, images, knowledges, affects, codes, habits, and practices" is produced. Second, in that the city is (and long has been) a site of aleatory, "joyful" encounter among singularities along the lines of Baudelaire's flâneur, as well as a site of insurgent political organization. And finally, in that the contemporary city is, like the factory, a site of exploitation, antagonism, conflict, and, hence, of potential rebellion. Leaving aside the urban–rural interdependencies and antagonisms that their account underplays, Hardt and Negri thereby recast the global or globalizing city as a "biopolitical city," a collective space of productive, life-or-death struggle against biopower, or the coercive management of everyday life.[13]

To illustrate, they single out rent as paradigmatic of the financialization of urban (or exurban) life: "Rent operates through a *desocialization of the common*, privatizing in the hands of the rich the common wealth produced and consolidated in the metropolis."[14] This contrasts land privatization not with public ownership, but with a common that exists beyond or outside of property relations and, hence, outside of such concepts as "private" or "public." Superficially, their argument shares some characteristics with Garrett Hardin's much-invoked "tragedy of the commons," but only in the inverse. Hardin, a biologist, argued in 1968 that the environmental commons, like the common agricultural lands that had been progressively enclosed as private (or public) property in Britain since the sixteenth century, is finite. The "tragedy" to which he refers is the proposition that the free pursuit of self-interest, such as increasing one's share in the land's output, inevitably leads to mutual loss. For Hardin, who assumes the all-powerful lawfulness of self-interest, the commons is therefore a "horror" to be abandoned in favor of privatization or administrative enclosure—what Arendt calls housekeeping—which he construes as lesser evils to that of resource depletion, figured mainly in the specter of overpopulation. That Hardin's most concrete proposal entails eugenic restrictions on the "freedom to breed" directed at the world's poorest populations, rather than an assault on poverty itself, is enough to remind us that here, too, biopower is at work.[15]

In contrast, Hardt and Negri construe the common as a sort of force field that overspills those processes that seek to expropriate it. They regard earlier collectivist projects such as socialism, with its state-centric language of "public" and "private," as philosophically if not practically distinct from what they call a "governance" of the common, accomplished through horizontal networks of democratic decision making by an autonomous, self-organizing multitude of singularities.

In a lively exchange, David Harvey has challenged their near-exclusive emphasis on these relational protocols over representative systems or other regimes of mediation. If the multitude is capable of commandeering biopolitical production toward revolutionary ends, "how," Harvey asks, "will this new value be represented and objectified in daily practice?"[16] Harvey reminds us, for example, that what Marx terms "fictitious capital" is value objectified as representation, or money, which recirculates in the form of securities and other higher-order financial abstractions. He is therefore asking, with some impatience: What will take the place of money, rent, and finance more generally—as representations of value—in the new forms of governance that Hardt and Negri envision? Rightly dismissing any romantic notion that conventional regimes might easily be abandoned ("don't tell me global bartering is feasible"), he implies that, like the socialist state or the communist international before it, the common requires institutions of its own, beginning with a medium of economic exchange.

Hardt and Negri certainly acknowledge as much. But they do not pre-empt this critique simply by suggesting that the abstractions of money and finance could, in principle, be turned against themselves to "provide the instruments for making the multitude from the diverse forms of flexible, mobile, and precarious labor."[17] Their direct reply to Harvey is that, whereas under industrial capitalism it may have been possible to regard economic production (labor and its products) as "real" and finance as "fictitious," "increasingly today the form of finance is symmetrical to the new processes of biopolitical production of value," such as codes, languages, and images. The project hence becomes one of "reappropriating socially what finance now possesses."[18]

What applies here to banks and financial institutions could presumably be said for other mediating institutions of the biopolitical commons, such as schools and universities, museums, libraries, laboratories, satellites, and so on. But how, exactly? Hardt and Negri insist repeatedly on the interdependence of revolutionary insurrection and patient institutional transformation, or of a Gramscian "war of movement" (or maneuver) and "war of position." On the side of institutions, they essentially ask: If socialist identification with the public and its cognates (the people, the proletariat, the state) has become ineffective or obsolete, what, if any, forms of networked mediation might enact globally a "democracy of the common" that is not one of surreptitious enclosure?

In response they argue that the pliable networks governing the neoliberal metropolis might be turned into both revolutionary instruments and genuinely democratic institutions. But, if this is possible, it is also possible that the ruined infrastructures of the socialist city be more closely interrogated for their transformative potential. From the point of view of the stagist model of history that Hardt and Negri rather too quickly adopt, public education, public health care, or public housing may indeed be vanishing into obsolescence. But these and other remnants of the socialist or reformist state remain very much part of the urban fabric and very much part of collective consciousness in many parts of the world. Emptied of their ideological force, these disused ruins *also* await reappropriation as instruments to redirect—to remediate, that is—the vectors of finance capital and its abstractions.

A Parable

In 1785, the French architect Etienne-Louis Boullée responded to a commission to relocate the Bibliothèque du Roi (Royal Library) to the Palace of the Louvre with one of his most well-known projects: a vast basilica-like reading room under a skylit vault, lined at its base with four tiers of books running entirely around its perimeter. In the immediate aftermath of the Revolution, the project to relocate the library was abandoned; the existing Royal Library was nationalized and became public, and the Palace became a museum. Boullée's proposal, which aligned despotic power with classical learning, has retroactively been celebrated as "revolutionary" for giving form to an Enlightenment republic of letters, the sort of communicational public sphere thought to be necessary for informed democratic citizenship, on a grand scale. Like the actually existing Royal/National Library, had it been realized, Boullée's project could possibly have functioned as such. It also could have functioned as an apparatus of state control, or as an archetypal medium of immaterial production. As is, it would be most accurate to regard the project as a ruined monument to monarchy that entered circulation as an enigmatic sign—that is, a non-fictitious unit of re-readable information that is now stored and circulated in books and silicon chips, which are in turn hooked up, rather uncannily in this case, to media complexes into which the project's dream of universal knowledge—and communication—has been tendentiously deformed.

Such media complexes are cobbled together from the leftover infrastructures of incomplete or obsolete sovereignties. As Marx famously said of revolutions, "The tradition of all the dead generations weighs like a nightmare on the brain of the living."[19] In Boullée's day a real palace, at the brink of revolution, begets an imaginary royal library, which in turn yields to a bourgeois state museum. Today, governments, corporations, and other bits and pieces of modernity combine to produce sovereign networks, all the nodes of which—including museums and libraries in the great metropolis, and satellites orbiting the earth—belong to the neoliberal republic of property. If another, common world is to be assembled outside these networks, it would necessarily include the richly textured ruins of the public, as a medium and as a message.

Notes

1. Hannah Arendt, *The Human Condition* (Chicago: University of Chicago Press, 1958), 50. On the *polis* and the "space of appearance," see 198–99.

2. Ibid., 57.

3. Jürgen Habermas, *The Structural Transformation of the Public Sphere: An Inquiry into a Category of Bourgeois Society* (1962), trans. Thomas Burger and Frederick Lawrence (Cambridge: MIT Press, 1989), 1–26. On the "reading public," see 43–56.

4. Nancy Fraser, "Rethinking the Public Sphere: A Contribution to the Critique of Actually Existing Democracy," in *Habermas and the Public Sphere*, ed. Craig Calhoun (Cambridge: MIT Press, 1992), 123.

5. Arendt, *The Human Condition*, 52.

6. Ibid., 1–6.

7. Michael Hardt and Antonio Negri, *Commonwealth* (Cambridge: Belknap Press of Harvard University Press, 2009), viii.

8. Michael Hardt and Antonio Negri, *Multitude: War and Democracy in the Age of Empire* (New York: Penguin, 2004), 204.

9. Hardt and Negri, *Commonwealth*, 273.

10. Ibid., 306–20, quote on 311.

11. Hardt and Negri, *Commonwealth*, 155.

12. Ibid., 249–50.

13. Ibid., 251–60.

14. Ibid., 258.

15. Garrett Hardin, "The Tragedy of the Commons," *Science* 162, no. 3859 (1968): 1243–48.

16. David Harvey, Michael Hardt, and Antonio Negri, "Commonwealth: An Exchange," *Artforum* 43, no. 3 (2009), 210–215, 256, 258, 269, 262; quote on 262.

17. Hardt and Negri, *Commonwealth*, 295.

18. Hardt and Negri, in Harvey, Hardt, and Negri, "Commonwealth," 215.

19. Karl Marx, *The Eighteenth Brumaire of Louis Bonaparte* (1852; repr., New York: International Publishers, 1963), 15.

[5]

Horizons of Thought

Earth is our commons. But it is also, after all, merely a locus, a locale. As if to remind us of this ineluctable fact, on August 25, 2012 or there-abouts, the Voyager 1 space probe left our solar system. We know this because on that Earthly day, the density of ionized plasma particles the probe encountered while hurtling through space decreased sharply, indicating that it had crossed the horizon created by the Sun's magnetic field.[1] That horizon forms the heliosphere, a plasma bubble within which our solar system is enclosed. Its radius is approximately 122 Astronomical Units (AUs). One AU is approximately 150 million kilometers in length, the average distance separating Earth from the Sun—which means that the radius of the heliosphere, and hence of the solar system, is roughly 18.3 billion kilometers.

Voyager 1 was launched by the American space agency NASA in 1977. Its primary mission had been to explore Jupiter and Saturn. In late 1980, after passing closely by Saturn's largest moon, Titan, which is of partic-ular scientific interest due to the atmospheric properties it is thought to share with the primeval Earth, the probe began its journey out of the solar system. As it did so, it continued to record observational data, the quantity of which was limited by the capacity of the probe's 1970s-style eight-track-tape storage bank. Nevertheless, NASA was able to extract suf-ficient data from the now-obsolete machine to confirm with relative con-fidence its historic crossing, which will likely be repeated in a few more years by its companion probe, Voyager 2.

Along with the data comes a certain melancholy. Unlike the ongoing exploration of Mars by NASA's Curiosity rover, or indeed, Voyager 1's ear-

lier encounter with Titan, both of which test the possibility of extrater-
restrial life or future human habitation, passage beyond the heliosphere
suggests little more than profound interstellar loneliness. The echoes
of anthropocentrism audible in references to Earthly scale, such as the
Earth-to-Sun metric of the Astronomical Unit, vanish like the dimin-
ishing signals from the probe's transmitter. Any remaining reference to
human experience, including the human life span or even humanity's
recorded history, is effectively cancelled by the realization that Voyager 1
will not encounter another star, or another solar system, for another forty
thousand years or so.

My purpose in recounting this story is twofold. First, it is to recall
the persistence of what the mid-twentieth century called the "measure
of man," or, the habit of describing space, even interplanetary space, in
terms relative to perceptible human scale and human experience. Second, it is to introduce the problem of the horizon in a manner that correlates that scale with certain untimely thoughts. "The time is out of joint"
was Jacques Derrida's way of anachronistically citing Shakespeare to conjure what he called the "specters of Marx" after the fall of the Berlin Wall.
In that spirit, I want to follow the path of Voyager and try, with the help of
another author, to conjure another time entirely, in order to gather some
lines that draw our historical present.

The year, this time, is 2026. The spaceship *Ares* carries a multicultural
group of one hundred scientists and engineers, plus one stowaway, on
a nine-month journey to colonize Mars. Kim Stanley Robinson's Mars
trilogy—*Red Mars, Green Mars,* and *Blue Mars*—does not quite begin with
this scene. Rather, it begins with the assassination some years later of the
colonists' charismatic leader and hints at the power struggle to follow.[2]
The books' titles, which encompass some 1,957 pages of intricate detail in
the best utopian tradition, refer to the different stages of Mars colonization: red, for the lifeless, geological purity of the planet as found, without
a viable atmosphere to speak of; green, for the network of verdant settlements that appear first under climate-controlled domes, and later, for the
gradual appearance of a manufactured, oxygenated atmosphere along
with the artificial thaw of polar ice, and the consequent spread of primal
vegetation genetically engineered to thrive in the harsh conditions; and
blue, for the final, planetary melt in a controlled deluge that produces
seas and continents, along with a comprehensive, Earthlike atmosphere

and weather, in which humans can at last live without prosthetic breathing devices or insulated suits.

This vastly accelerated process of warming the red planet, wrapping it in oxygen and nitrogen, and propagating animal and vegetal species, is called "terraforming." It is the source of most, if not all, of the planet's political turmoil over the course of the three volumes. Terraforming is a science fiction staple, with some basis in extant techniques for what is known as geoengineering. Of the story's main characters, whose intertwined lives the narrative follows, nearly all are members or offspring of this "first hundred." Each character figures metonymically, or allegorizes, a distinct political shade or position relative to the terraforming process. Many move in and out of the twenty-plus Martian political parties, either as leaders or as charismatic symbols. At one pole of the political debate are the fundamentalist "Reds," who want at all costs to conserve the planet's barren geology in its primal state; at the other pole are the developmentalist "Greens," who advocate "viriditas," or the inexorable proliferation of life. Both have quasi-theological dimensions. The most extreme "Reds," figured in the renegade geologist Ann Clayborne, practice a monastic asceticism devoted to the primal beauty of the planet's barren surface, while the more devout "Greens" hew to a cult of viriditas led by Hiroko Ai, a guru-like bioengineer.

Crisscrossing the red–green polarity is a myriad of other, this-not-that dialectical oppositions. These include nested movements between the secular and the religious, between the rational and the irrational, between pure and applied science, between male and female, and even a somewhat fudged dialectic between capitalism and communism. Each axis in this multidimensional matrix brings its own subplots and contradictions, beginning with the ambiguous political valence of the colors "red" and "green" themselves (despite Robinson's manifest debt to Alexander Bogdanov's *Red Star* of 1908). But the trilogy's dialectic is incomplete without the Mars–Earth axis itself, materialized in the great space elevator installed on Mars at which space shuttles dock in orbit to discharge their loads in order to ease the energy demands of interplanetary travel imposed by gravity and atmospheric friction—before, that is, the entire structure winds up wrapped twice around the planet following an act of revolutionary sabotage that takes it down and reorients the narrative toward a violently contested future.

I feel comfortable in referring to the dialectical structure of this popular science fiction series because, for one, its author, Kim Stanley Robinson, holds a Ph.D. in English from the University of California at San Diego and is well schooled in dialectical thought. His doctoral thesis, which he completed in 1982, analyzed the novels of Philip K. Dick; among his mentors was the Marxian literary theorist Fredric Jameson.

Robinson credits Jameson with introducing him to Marxism and to literary theory.[3] In turn, Jameson has written about Robinson's work, most notably in the concluding chapter of his *Archaeologies of the Future: The Desire Called Utopia and Other Science Fictions* (2005). The title of that chapter, which was first published in 2000, is "'If I Find One Good City I'll Spare the Man': Realism and Utopia in Kim Stanley Robinson's Mars Trilogy."[4] For Jameson, the realism indicated in his subtitle is exemplified by one of the trilogy's central characters, the problem-solving scientific polymath Sax Russell, for whom, as Jameson puts it, "external reality organizes itself into a problem" to which science responds. But at some level, at some point, the scientific solution or explanation encounters a limit, thus presenting what Jameson calls a "resistance." Scientific knowledge emerges dialectically out of this resistance, while remaining ontologically bounded by what Robinson's scientist hero calls "the great unexplainable."[5] The obdurate resistance of reality to comprehensive explanation is both generative and secular. Following the more conventional arc of descriptive literary realisms, which, as in architecture and the visual arts, are commonly said to have been superseded by abstract, reflexive modernism, this resistance is gradually shown, according to Jameson, to be a novelistic conceit. It is a fiction comparable to the impenetrable puzzle erected at the outset of a mystery novel only to be solved by the novel's end. Modernism turns the tables on this type of realism by examining reflexively how it is produced, in the process upending narrative, figuration, and representation. However, even at its most dogmatic, a modernist (and eventually postmodernist) attention to the constructedness of realist narratives, and ultimately of scientific facts, does not automatically cancel or relativize the underlying reality, as simplistic critiques of poststructuralist theory would have it. Instead, it raises that reality to the second degree. As Jameson puts it, still referring indirectly to the pages and pages of scientific and para-scientific description packed into Robinson's Mars trilogy: "Behind the theory of social construction, therefore, lies praxis and human production itself, which makes a mockery of realism's staged mystery stories."[6] In short, Mars is a mirror.

Terraforming, in this formulation, is a dialectical procedure by which *both* a particular, a priori reality—Martian geology—and its potential human constructions come into view, rather than simply replacing one order of being (geological, primal, "red") with another (biological, cultural, "green"). To this dialectic Jameson adds the Earth–Mars axis. For him, that axis secures the properly utopian character of Robinson's series, as the dystopia of progressively dire conditions on Earth and the resulting interplanetary migration put increased pressure on the fragile Martian ecosystem. The space elevator, its destruction, replacement, and eventual multiplication, together with the 54.6 million kilometers separating the two planetary orbits and the variety of techno–social arrangements devised to span the distance, is the structural equivalent of the geo-engineered trench separating the island of Utopia from the mainland in Thomas More. An asymmetrical back and forth runs between a still recognizable Earth, ruled by "metanational" corporations and weak states and subject to extreme global warming and overpopulation, and, following a second revolution, an agonistically democratic and pluralistic Mars. The ensuing Earth–Mars relationship is, however, only apparently dichotomous. Not only does the red–green dialectic reflexively mirror the terms of actually existing environmental politics on today's Earth; the fictional interplay of utopia and dystopia, elaborated in matter-of-fact, realist prose, reflexively marks the limits and blind spots of those same politics. Within this schema, in the trilogy, the literal and figurative distance from Earth elicits for Jameson the cognitive estrangement necessary to achieve on Mars what he calls a "polyphonic" utopianism, or "a struggle between a whole range of utopian alternatives, about which [the trilogy] deliberately fails to conclude."[7]

Jameson concludes by naming the mysterious abolition of money as the narrative's most basic, unexplained—and therefore overdetermined—utopian premise. However, neither he nor Robinson directly take up what is arguably the trilogy's more vexing epistemological problem. Among its tour de force technological conceits, described in exhaustive para-scientific detail, are the exploitation of the Martian planet's geology and hydrology, the epic harnessing of solar energy with a giant space mirror, the mining of satellites, the chemical construction of an atmosphere, and even the evolution of a new quasi-species of taller, more agile humans in the diminished Martian gravity. However, given all the detailed technical invention elsewhere, arguably more mysterious even than the abolition of money is the existence of something called the "gerontological treatments," or merely the "treatments." These treatments, which have to be re-administered every few decades, virtually eliminate disease and prolong human life by an unknown extent, which is thought to be hundreds or even thousands of years. Two of the original Mars scientist–colonists were instrumental in their development and implementation. From the outset, the longevity treatments are the basis for a socioeconomic apartheid that rebounds racially, gradually constructing two competing categories of humans. On Earth, access to the treatments requires either considerable private means, membership in "metanational" corporate life (which provides them as a sort of employee benefit), or status as a Mars colonist. Anyone without such access is condemned to live entirely outside the sphere in which the trilogy's principal contest between "red" and "green" utopias occurs.

Vastly increased longevity, even for a minority of Earth's population, leads quickly to a massive population explosion and, hence, political pressure to increase Mars migration quotas, particularly from large countries like India and China and their corporate patrons. These migrations in turn threaten the Martian ecology, an effect that generates profound political struggle on Mars and is opposed with particular vehemence by the red planet's conservationist faction. In this sense, the Earth–Mars axis poses what Friedrich Engels called the "housing question" at the planetary scale of mass migration, but displaces it onto the ecological plane. Meanwhile, back on Earth, the situation becomes critical when a subterranean volcanic eruption fractures and melts the West Antarctic ice cap, flooding coastal cities and dramatically accelerating the greenhouse effect, resulting in full-scale planetary warming.

Somewhat less remarked however by either Robinson or Jameson are the more immediate consequences of the apartheid, and in particular, the biomedical (and hence biopolitical) divisions that it engenders. The starkest division, separating those who have received the treatments from those who have not, potentially leads to more sustained human precariousness than do the divisions separating inland populations from coastal ones after the deluge, or indeed, Earth from Mars. In this respect, the epic red–green struggle that unfolds in the Mars trilogy *as well as its peaceful resolution* are based on a prior distinction between the radically extended species-being of those who might live a thousand years, and the radically attenuated species-being of those who will not. Nor is life span the sole consequence of the new order, for the biomedical apartheid incites a whole range of peripheral conflicts. Countries and metanational managers face intense pressure from below to address their underserved populations, who include both the ageless generations piling up in over-crowded cities and towns, and the *lumpenproletariat* of the untreated, ever present just over the horizon. But when revolution occurs, it occurs on Mars, not on Earth, and not as a result of these raw conflicts but, ostensi-bly at least, as a separatist fight over ecological custody of the planet and its resources that devolves into a civil war among two groups—the "Reds" and the "Greens"—who have already benefitted from the longevity treat-ments and are therefore able to participate in the utopian project in the first place.

In this sense, the Earthly (or Terran) biopolitical conflict over access to the treatments inverts the terms of the Martian ecological conflict of development versus conservation. On Earth, those who remain closest, medically speaking, to the biological state of nature, are at risk of even-tually being classified as subhuman in relation to those who have had full access to the longevity treatments. What is most natural is therefore most precarious. Meanwhile on Mars, the conservationist, naturalist impera-tive is repeatedly invoked as a moral ideal by those already treated. The changing horizontal stratum at the crest of the planet's new atmosphere sets the mark, below which is "green" construction, and above which is "red" nature.

Thus, the entire dialectic of "red" conservationist utopias and "green" developmentalist ones—Mars as a test, a lesson for Earth—depends on the partition of the human species into two: those who have access to the longevity treatments and those who do not. The first, treated group participates in the test, and hence in the contradictions and reflexivity of utopian thought along the doubled-up Earth–Mars, red–green axes; the second, untreated group does not, by virtue of having been written out the equation—and indeed the story—almost entirely. Just as the aboli-tion of money is described but not fully accounted for in the series, the eventual erasure of this divide, with the full Terran population gradu-ally gaining access to the treatments, is noted but not explained. Is this the final triumph of the realist utopia, in which problem-solving scientific enterprise finally domesticates obdurate nature, including the nature of life itself, and transcends the resistance of the political with its solutions? Or is it the opposite: the triumph of the real—of politics, in the form of structural exclusion—over even the most dialectically uncompromising, plural, and "polyphonic" utopia?

By "real" here I do not mean natural. I mean prior, preexisting, in the sense that the biomedical, biopolitical apartheid I have been describing preexists and supports the manifest political content of Robinson's three books. What is real about it is not the scientific or biological plausibility of the gerontological treatments, or even the way in which these mimic or allegorize similar divisions among actually existing Earthlings, as when Robinson rather offhandedly describes the splendid touristic isolation of one native Martian visiting the picturesque ruins of Crete: "The rest of Earth, however, was Calcutta."[8] What is real about the biomedical apartheid is the way it circumscribes or limits the political allegory of the Mars trilogy. The apartheid is not in itself dialectical; it marks an a priori horizon, internal to the narrative yet only partially acknowledged by it, which makes the dialectics of "utopia" and "realism" possible in the first place.

Elsewhere, Jameson has persuasively argued that the true vocation of utopian thought is not to think Utopia, but to reveal its very unthinkability under present conditions. The question is therefore not simply "What must change?" but rather "What must change so that change will be thinkable?" Hence, the most forcefully utopian question posed by the Mars trilogy is not "Red or green?" or even "Earth or Mars?" It is: How could this be? How could the dialectic of utopia and realism, and hence the mirror/model that is Mars, be built on another, even more stark reality that passes nearly unnoticed by the dialectic?

Which returns us to where we began, with Voyager's exit from the heliosphere. Among the most fantastical sections of the Mars trilogy are those in the third book, *Blue Mars,* which describe the further colonization of the outer solar system. There, Mars's original pluralism is multiplied into the diverse characteristics imposed on various terraforming missions by the specific geological, meteorological, and atmospheric conditions of the other planets and their satellites, and in the myriad technological, cultural, and political–economic responses to these conditions. Among the most architecturally innovative is a Superstudio-like continuous monument known as Terminator that glides slowly along tracks wrapping Mercury's equator, its imperceptible, steady movement propelled by the differential expansion of the tracks when exposed to the sun's intense heat as the planet rotates, keeping the city just beyond the

horizon in permanent, protective shadow. Others include Jupiter's aster-
oid belt, which now contains mines and settlements carved into individual asteroids, as well as the four big Jovian moons, known as the Galileans:
Callisto, Ganymede, Io, and Europa, all with massive illumination projects to compensate for the minimal direct sunlight they receive. Still
another is the restless settler colony on Oberon, one of Uranus's moons,
whose inhabitants already have their sights set on Pluto and its largest
satellite, Charon.

Indeed, by the conclusion of the third book the entire solar system
has become to Mars what Mars had been to Earth—a colonial frontier in
which are reflected all the aspirations, conflicts, and ideological struggles
of the home planet. Now, however, these are no longer spread in microcosm in small settlements across the Martian landscape. They are spread
in macrocosm across the solar system itself.

More recently, in the quasi-sequel *2312*, Robinson has explored the
ensuing "balkanization" via an interplanetary whodunit-cum-romance
that begins in Mercury's Terminator and ricochets around the solar system.[9] Mixed in with Martian, Venusian, Saturnine, Jovian, and Mercurial
provincialisms and interdependencies, as well as a whole solar system's
worth of communitarian tensions and alliances, is again the underlying
biomedical apartheid, which now separates genetically modified, sexually
hybridized "spacers" from multitudinous, untreated Earthlings. Periodi-
cally, the narrative dwells on the persistent and growing gulf between the
two, such as when a protagonist passes through a subaltern (and partially
submerged) Jersey City and picks up a refugee who, arriving on Venus,
becomes pivotal to the story—a story that rehearses a primary, non-
dialectical partition imposed on the human species by itself, an internal
horizon that the refugee, and only the refugee, crosses.

This is where the reality of Voyager 1, having crossed the gaseous frontier and left to hurtle through the interstellar void, joins the utopianism
of the Mars trilogy. As a scientific probe, its weakening signals, stored on
eight-track tape, continue to record human encounter with the material universe, in a fashion as realist as any of Robinson's fictional scientist
heroes. But its hidden utopianism does not lie in the distant promise of
one day populating the solar system with human settlements, a promise
that, as the Mars trilogy reminds us, merely lays out for inspection all the
conflicts and contradictions of present-day Earthly existence. Nor does
its utopianism lie in the promise of yet farther horizons. Its utopianism,

which is also its realism, lies in what it conceals as much as what it reveals: that the horizons of thought are where the sky and the ground meet. These horizons encompass the 122 Astronomical Units that now separate us from Voyager. All of human history is contained in that distance, as is the inability to see simultaneously the starry skies and the ground on which we stand. Both are real, but, as the Mars trilogy also implies, truly utopian thought recognizes that the question of how to inhabit the skies is *preceded* by the question of how to inhabit the Earth, rather than alternative to it. Utopia, then, is a down-to-earth thought, as mundane and unexciting as reopening the housing question.

When Hannah Arendt began *The Human Condition* with the image of the Sputnik satellite orbiting the Earth, she observed that the event was greeted in the American press by "relief" about what one report called a "step toward escape from men's imprisonment to the [E]arth." Recognizing that in Sputnik, science had merely realized and ratified ordinary dreams, "neither wild nor idle," that had theretofore been restricted to the "the highly non-respectable literature of science fiction," she warned that "the banality of the statement should not make us overlook how extraordinary in fact it was."[10] Leaving aside the overtones of another "banality" (Arendt, of course, would later write of the "banality of evil" in reference to the perpetrators of the Holocaust), her emphasis on the ordinariness of the sentiment is striking.

It is with some irony, then, that history has turned the tables, and led us down a path in which the extraordinary has become an all-enveloping fact, a planetary prison of our own making. In the past decade or so, scientists and some historians have begun to characterize the period since 1800 as marking the threshold of the Anthropocene, a new geological epoch defined by the vastly expanded impact of human civilizational activity on the biological, chemical, and physical matter of the Earth. They have argued that the period begins with the first phase of industrialization in Europe and in North America, which, by extension, includes industrial capitalism, the nation-state, modern imperialism, the expansion of the slave trade, and the institutionalization of the human sciences and the natural sciences, among other things.[11] All of these historical processes and many more have played their role in human-induced, or anthropogenic, changes to the Earth's systems that now threaten what Marx called, in a moment of underappreciated foresight, humanity's "species-being."

To limit the damage, some scientists have proposed establishing "planetary boundaries" specific to critical biological and physiochemical processes.[12] Allowing environmental change to cross these boundaries risks condemning Earth and its inhabitants to a profoundly uncertain and perilous future. Optimistically, Robinson's books tell of an escape from such boundaries, if only to find new, even more fragile ones elsewhere, as settlers struggle violently over whether and how to replicate Earth's ecosystems on a geoengineered Mars. Meanwhile, imprisoned on the other end of the Earth–Mars axis, and reflecting of the prospect of a terraformed Earth as a means of reversing the effects of climate change, Robinson describes his work as an attempt "to write the realism of the 21st century."[13] But even as we acknowledge the reflexivity of Mars-as-mirror, we might prefer to consider the Mars trilogy as a counterhistory. On the one hand, the narrative is replete with techniques for rebalancing Earth's systems that might awaken, in a dialectical fashion, a planetary consciousness adequate to the scale of the anthropogenic crisis. On the other hand, its particular form of utopianism vividly shows Earth's internal divisions, blind spots, and horizons being reproduced externally. In so doing, the trilogy, like Voyager's weakening signal transmitted with obsolete hardware, reminds us that where we are going both is and is not where we have been. The ordinariness of this extraordinary fact, which has quietly presided over the centuries in which modernity has unfolded, might cause us, in the spirit of science fictions long gone, to "look backward" at ourselves looking forward, if only to realize that it is here that the real horizons lie.

Notes

1. Brook Barnes, "In a Breathtaking First, NASA's Voyager 1 Exits the Solar System," *New York Times*, September 12, 2013, http://www.nytimes.com/2013/09/13/science/in-a-breathtaking-first-nasa-craft-exits-the-solar-system.html. See also D. A. Gurnett et al., "In Situ Observations of Interstellar Plasma with Voyager 1," *Science* 217, vol. 341, no. 6153 (2013): 1489–92. Also Andrew Grant, "At Last, Voyager 1 Slips into Interstellar Space," *Science News*, September 12, 2013, http://www.sciencenews.org/view/generic/id/353199/description/At_last_Voyager_1_slips_into_interstellar_space.

2. Kim Stanley Robinson, *Red Mars* (New York: Bantam, 1993), *Green Mars* (New York: Bantam, 1994), *Blue Mars* (New York: Bantam, 1996).

3. Imre Szeman and Maria Whiteman, "Future Politics: An Interview with Kim Stanley Robinson," *Science Fiction Studies* 31, no. 93 (2004), http://www.depauw.edu/sfs/interviews/robinson93interview.htm.

4. Fredric Jameson, "'If I Find One Good City I'll Spare the Man': Realism and Utopia in Kim Stanley Robinson's Mars Trilogy," in *Archaeologies of the Future: The Desire Called Utopia and Other Science Fictions* (New York: Verso, 2005), 393–416.

5. Ibid., 397–98.

6. He continues: "Production, praxis, even construction as such, in fact require the resistance of some initial raw material, diffused through the situation which itself takes shape under the pickaxe of the original project: it is a formula that combines both requirements, that of the confrontation of an unyielding set of elements, to be inventoried and described, that of the human pressure that will gradually give them names and the appearance, if not yet of a city, at least of its quarry and foundation pit, an immense building site whose skyline is still unknown." Ibid., 400.

7. Ibid., 410. As the narrative progresses, this estrangement increasingly defines the oscillation between the Earthly dystopia and what Jameson calls the "'realm of freedom' which is the Martian public sphere." Ibid., 413.

8. Robinson, *Blue Mars*, 500.

9. Kim Stanley Robinson, *2312* (New York: Orbit, 2012).

10. Arendt, *The Human Condition*, 1–2.

11. Will Steffen, Jacques Grinevald, Paul Crutzen, and John McNeill, "The Anthropocene: Conceptual and Historical Perspectives," *Philosophical Transactions of the Royal Society* A 369 (2011): 842–67; Dipesh Chakrabarty, "The Climate of History: Four Theses," *Critical Inquiry* 35, no. 2 (2009): 197–222.

12. Johann Rockström et al., "Planetary Boundaries: Exploring the Safe Operating Space for Humanity," *Ecology and Society* 14, no. 2 (2009), http://www.ecologyandsociety.org/vol14/iss2/art32/.

13. Kim Stanley Robinson, "Terraforming Earth," *Slate*, December 4, 2012, http://www.slate.com/articles/health_and_science/onearth/2012/12/geoengineering_science_fiction_and_fact_kim_stanley_robinson_on_how_we_are.html.

Acknowledgments

Although it may be premature to attach acknowledgments to a work-in-progress, I want to express my gratitude to those whose invitations prompted initial versions of the five essays included here: Edurne Portela at the Lehigh University Humanities Center, Peter van der Veer at the Max Planck Institute for the Study of Ethnic and Religious Diversity, Richard Birkett and Sam Lewitt at the Museum moderner Kunst Stiftung Ludwig Wien, Nancy Levinson at *Places*, and Ljiljana Blagojević at the University of Belgrade. Many others have contributed thoughts and insights to which these essays react. I am especially grateful to all the students who have participated in my seminar "Philosophies of the City" at Columbia University, where I first had the opportunity to formulate many of the reflections developed here. Phillip Wegner offered an astute reading of the draft manuscript to which I have tried to do justice; more informally, Andreas Huyssen advised on an early version of chapter 3. Finally, I thank Danielle Kasprzak, Pieter Martin, and Mike Stoffel at the University of Minnesota Press for their farsightedness and for their support.

About the Author

Reinhold Martin is professor of architecture at Columbia University. He cofounded the journal *Grey Room* and is the author of *Utopia's Ghost: Architecture and Postmodernism, Again* (Minnesota, 2010) and *The Organizational Complex: Architecture, Media, and Corporate Space*.